The Psychological Effects of Police Work

A Psychodynamic Approach

CRIMINAL JUSTICE AND PUBLIC SAFETY

Series Editor: Philip John Stead
John Jay College of Criminal Justice
The City University of New York
New York, New York

The Psychological Effects of Police Work

A Psychodynamic Approach

Philip Bonifacio
John Jay College of Criminal Justice
City University of New York
New York, New York

Plenum Press • New York and London

Library of Congress Cataloging-in-Publication Data

Bonifacio, Philip.
    The psychological effects of police work : a psychodynamic
approach / Philip Bonifacio.
        p.   cm. -- (Criminal justice and public safety)
    Includes bibliographical references and index.
    ISBN 0-306-43955-7
    1. Police--United States. 2. Law enforcement--United States-
-Psychological aspects. 3. Police psychology.   I. Title.
II. Series.
HV8138.B557 1991
363.2'01'9--dc20
                                                         91-27753
                                                              CIP

ISBN 0-306-43955-7

© 1991 Plenum Press, New York
A Division of Plenum Publishing Corporation
233 Spring Street, New York, N.Y. 10013

Printed in the United States of America

To the memory of
Anthony Bonifacio
and
Rose Bonifacio

and to

Richard Koller,
who started me
wondering what
was going on

Preface

SOME DISCLAIMERS

It is somewhat unusual to begin a book by declaring what it is not, but the topic of police behavior is so complex that it requires the writer to state as early as possible the limits of what he has written here to describe and explain a police officer's experience. In order for the reader to get a clear idea of what areas of police behavior are to be described, it is necessary to delineate those aspects of police behavior that are beyond the scope of this book.

First of all, this book is about the psychological effects of police work on policemen: male police officers. Nearly all of the police officers with whom I have worked have been men, so my impressions and opinions are based on the experiences of male police officers. Consequently, descriptions and explanations of the motivations, anxieties, psychological defenses, and resultant behavior of police officers must be limited to policemen. I believe that there are significant differences in the psychological effects of police work on men and women, but this book does not address this issue.

The second limitation of this book is that formulations to understand the psychological effects of the job are based on the experiences of policemen in large, urban police departments. There are fundamental differences in the effects of urban and rural police work that make generalizations from the psychological experiences of urban officers to those of rural officers tenuous at best and inaccurate at worst. For example, the urban policeman is anonymous to the civilian population and is therefore more readily made into a fantasy figure by civilians. On the other hand the rural police officer is known by most of the civilians, often on a first-name basis. There is far less fantasy created about who he is because civilians know him as a person as well as a policeman. While the rural officer may have fewer problems with being seen as a caricature, he does have more difficulty maintaining his authority with civilians who know him personally (Zamble & Annesley, 1987).

Another significant difference between the psychological effects of urban and rural police work is the officer's relationship with the police department. To the urban officer, the department is a largely remote yet powerful force with which he must contend. In many ways the police department as an institution is as anonymous to him as he is to civilians in the street. The department's anonymity fosters a great deal of fantasizing by the policeman about its power and its treatment of him. The rural police officer may know every member of his department and have an accurate impression of the personalities of the senior administrators. So the impetus to create fantasies about "the department" and "the chiefs" may not be very great for the rural policeman. These two examples illustrate why this book's descriptions and interpretations of a policeman's psychological experience may not apply to rural officers.

A third limitation of this book is that it takes only one view—the psychodynamic view—to describe a policeman's experience and behavior. Those who write from the psychodynamic perspective are often accused of dismissing or at least minimizing the importance of other approaches, such as the cognitive, sociological, and organizational views, in understanding the totality of human behavior. This accusation often has merit. With that in mind, my intention is that the psychodynamic view will complement—not replace—other theoretical approaches in describing and understanding the psychological impact of police work.

There is no such thing as *the* definitive explanation for human behavior. There can only be ongoing attempts from many positions to differentiate behavior into its significant components, which will ultimately lead to an integration of these components into a meaningful and comprehensible whole. The behavioral sciences are in the initial stage of differentiating police behavior and therefore are in need of as many viewpoints as possible. This book offers the psychodynamic approach as one more viewpoint, certainly not the only one.

Finally, this book does not view a policeman's psychological experience and behavior as either pathological or well adjusted. The psychodynamic view assumes that behavior, *all* behavior, "normal" and "abnormal," results from the interaction of "identifiable psychological factors that are often in conflict and are powerful, usually unconscious, always influential motivating forces of human behavior" (Paolino, 1981, p. 16). This assumption says that behavior is the resultant compromise of opposing forces in the unconscious part of a person's mind, so that these unconscious forces affect behavior without the person being aware of them. This assumption holds for everyone's behavior—police and civilian, normal, neurotic and psychotic.

The psychodynamic position believes that what you see is *not* what you get when it comes to behavior. There are always unseen motives underlying observable behavior that must be detected and understood if we are to explain the behavior we see. The psychodynamic view also says that once you examine underlying motives for behavior, no one comes out looking like a saint and almost no one comes out looking like a complete villain. This book will attempt to describe the conflicting, often unconscious forces that result in observed behavior of policemen. In examining these forces, the officer is regarded not as either martyr or sadist, but as human. Just like the rest of us, the police officer grapples with his impulses, his emotions, his conscience, and his external environment. And just like the rest of us, his behavior is the result of his attempts to cope with all these factors.

This view of police behavior brings us to the fourth limitation of this book: it cannot and will not make everyone totally happy with what it says. The "cop lover" will not like some of the interpretations of his hero worship of the police officer as based on an unconscious wish to see the cop as a loving father. Similarly, the "cop hater" will resent the explanation for his hatred as the result of an unconscious need to see the cop as a cruel parent.

The police establishment will not like to read that it sends mixed messages of love and hate to the policeman, which cause him considerable anxiety. The police fraternity will not be pleased with the interpretation that it is both emotionally supportive and yet highly punitive in its treatment of the individual policeman. The policeman's wife and children may be distressed by the description of their mixed feelings of love and hate for him. And the police officer himself may feel anxious about interpretations of his mixed feelings for everyone else—the public, the department, his family and brother officers—and also for the work itself.

Since the psychodynamic approach to behavior seeks not to condemn or condone but to understand, the positions taken in this book are attempts to explain rather than to take sides.

OBJECTIVES

This book has several objectives. The first is to make the policeman aware of the complex influences of the job on his unconscious mind and his emotions. I hope that with greater understanding of the forces that influence what he feels, thinks, and does, the police officer will have the chance to develop effective ways of coping with them.

The second goal is to make all those who have an emotional impact on the police officer—civilians, the police department, his wife and children, his friends, and fellow police officers—be more aware of their own mixed feelings toward him and of how their feelings affect the officer's emotional and behavioral reactions to them.

Third, this book seeks to generate further interest and research in the psychodynamic aspects of police work, an area I believe is of vital importance if we are to have a better understanding of problems such as stress, job satisfaction, marital problems, abnormal behavior, and deviance among police. This area has been largely ignored because it does not lend itself to quantitative research methods and is a politically sensitive issue in law enforcement.

Finally, it is hoped that mental health professionals who work with policemen will include the psychodynamic view of their assessment and treatment of police officers. While approaches like biofeedback and behavior modification certainly have a place in the psychological treatment of officers, they cannot be expected to be the universal treatments of choice.

OVERVIEW

Chapter 1 covers a theoretical overview of the psychodynamic approach to human behavior, especially the influence of ambivalence, the simultaneous feeling of love and hate. Chapter 2 describes how the policeman is subjected to ambivalence from the public, the police department, his family and friends, and from other police officers. Chapter 3 explores the policeman's own ambivalent feelings toward the public, the department, his family and friends, and other policemen. The policeman's love and hate for the job itself is examined in Chapter 4. I believe that this is probably the most important part of the book since it deals with the most fundamental psychological aspects of the police officer's experience. His love and hatred for the work have virtually nothing to do with anyone else. They come solely from unconscious conflicting forces within himself.

The policeman's attempts to cope with the ambivalence of others and with his own ambivalence, and the resultant behavior caused by these coping devices, are discussed in Chapter 5. The role of defense mechanisms as coping devices is described in terms of how they are employed and the observable behavior that results from them. We then shift gears in Chapter 6 in which various issues in police work described in the literature are examined from a psychodynamic point of view. Issues such as police stress, the police personality, the myths of the "dumb cop," corruption, and brutality will be examined with respect to the role of unconscious forces on them.

Clinical issues in police work are covered in Chapter 7. Alcohol abuse, suicide, marital problems, trauma, and line-of-duty injuries are examined in terms of the underlying emotional influences of the job on these problems and on the defenses used by the officer to cope with them. In Chapter 8, suggestions for dealing with the pervasive influence of ambivalence on the police officer are presented along with explanations as to why they may be difficult—if not impossible—to implement.

It is hoped that as the reader progresses through these chapters and for whatever reason feels anxious or angry in self-defense, that he or she bear in mind that the policeman is not regarded here as superman or sadist, but as an ordinary human being subjected to highly extraordinary emotional experiences that have a powerful impact on him. If we civilians are to see the policeman as a human being rather than as the embodiment of virtue or evil, we must recognize and understand those forces in us that make us see him as either superman or less than human. If police officers are to view themselves as human rather than as superheroes or society's victims, they must also recognize and understand those same forces that make them see themselves as different from everyone else.

Acknowledgments

This book would still be just an idea without the encouragement and assistance of colleagues, friends, and family. Thanks to Dr. Ron McVey for believing in the idea, encouraging me to put it on paper, and contacting John Stead on my behalf. I am grateful to John Stead, editor of the Criminal Justice and Public Safety series of Plenum Press, for his patience and tolerance of my anxiety and procrastination, and for his continual encouragement.

Special thanks are given to Patricia Sinatra, my colleague, friend, editor, reviewer, typist, and occasional taskmaster. Her encouragement, assistance, and gentle tongue-lashings to keep working were essential to this book's becoming a reality.

I am very grateful to George Best, Frank Marousek, Dr. William McCarthy, and Dr. H. Bruce Pierce for their support and invaluable contributions. Thanks also to Marvie Brooks, librarian at John Jay College, for her patience and diligence in tracking down esoteric journal articles.

Finally, I thank my wife, Adrianne, and my daughter, Elena, for their understanding and patience while I spent so many weekends holed up at the computer.

Contents

Chapter 1

An Overview of the Psychodynamic Approach

Human beings like to congratulate themselves for their capacity to use reason and to behave logically. Reason, we like to tell ourselves, is what separates us from animals. We regard our behavior as the product of the application of logic in our daily lives, and see our minds as not merely guided by reason but dominated by it. As a result we are superior to other animals precisely because our intellect is firmly grounded in the rules of logic and our behavior is based on the application of those rules.

This self-image of man as a purely logical organism is both self-serving and incorrect. We are dominated by much more than the forces of logic. A great deal of what we think, feel, say and do is directed by something other than the cool application of reason. Any policeman who has worked in the street will tell you that people can say and do an incredible number of illogical and unreasonable things. He knows that

1

something other than logic influences the thoughts and actions of people, even the average, law-abiding ones.

THE UNCONSCIOUS

The psychodynamic approach to behavior believes that
there is more than just conscious logic that motivates people
to think and act in certain ways. Behavior is the result of unconscious as well as conscious mental forces. These unconscious forces are collectively labeled "the unconscious." The
unconscious, as we shall discuss in the section on the structure
of the mind (p. 16), does not operate according to reason and
the rules of logic, but according to its own nonlogical principles. As a result, the unconscious has immunity from reason,
so that it cannot be understood by employing a purely logical
approach.

In addition to the principle of unconscious motivation,
the psychodynamic approach believes that there is no such
thing as chance behavior. One's thoughts, words, and deeds
are not random occurrences, but are the result of some cause,
either conscious or unconscious. Since behavior never simply
occurs, then there must always be a motive for it. So, if
thoughts, feelings, or actions do not seem to have a ready
explanation, it is not because there is none. It is that their
underlying cause may be in large measure unconscious.

THE CONSCIOUS AND UNCONSCIOUS PARTS OF
THE MIND

The psychodynamic view of behavior sees the human
mind as a kind of iceberg. Only 10 percent of an iceberg is
above the water and therefore easy to detect. The other 90
percent is below the water, invisible to the eye. To understand
the iceberg's true dimensions, you have to go below the
water's surface to examine what you can of the hidden 90

percent. Like the visible tip of the iceberg, the part of our mind that is readily accessible to observation and guided by logic is only a small part of the complex structure of the mind. This observable, logical component is called our "conscious mind." We can study the conscious mind by administering tests of intelligence, perception, and problem solving, and we can do a fairly good job of describing its characteristics. In fact, computers can now simulate human intelligence in solving complicated tasks.

The other part of the mind, the unconscious, is below the surface of our conscious awareness and is not directly observable. We know it is there because we can observe certain forms of human behavior that do not seem to be logical or directed by reason. Brenner (1973) give five examples to demonstrate the existence of the unconscious. First, under hypnosis a person can be given posthypnotic suggestions, which are actually directions to perform specific actions after being brought out of his or her "trance." After being awakened the individual will perform these actions without being able to explain why he or she is doing them (Brenner, 1973). The subject has no conscious awareness of the cause of his or her behavior. "Such an experiment," says Brenner, "shows clearly that a truly unconscious mental process (obedience to a command in this case) can have a dynamic or motive effect on thought and behavior" (1973, p. 11).

Dreams are a second example of the existence of the unconscious part of the mind. Although not awake while dreaming, the individual experiences the dream's sensory images. We experience the images in a dream that are produced by our unconscious mind. For example, when starving men dream of "gorging themselves at banquets, they are not conscious of hunger but of [eating]" (Brenner, 1973, p. 11), so that their unconscious mind produced dream images of eating. The dream that satisfied their wish to eat came from their unconscious rather than their conscious mind. To paraphrase Jiminy Cricket, a dream is a wish your unconscious gratifies when you are fast asleep.

Another example of the existence of the unconscious and its influence on the conscious mind are the everyday slips of the tongue and memory lapses. Calling a new girlfriend by the old girlfriend's name, forgetting the name of someone you do not like when making introductions, and writing a check for the wrong amount (invariably too small) are indications that behavior is influenced by unconscious forces as well as conscious ones. These errors are caused by unconscious wishes that override our conscious directives.

The fourth example has to do with people revealing their motives to everyone else while being unable to see their motives themselves. For example, a man may be very competitive in his behavior, so much so that it is obvious to everyone else, and yet remain unaware of his competitive motives. Not only will he deny these feelings, he will be surprised and hurt that so many people misunderstand him. This example shows how unconscious impulses can have a profound effect on one's behavior while remaining outside the person's conscious awareness.

The fifth illustration of the presence and influence of the unconscious part of the mind is the neurotic symptom. It is now axiomatic in psychotherapy to conclude that a person's symptom is a behavioral representation of an unconscious wish in disguised form. As Brenner points out, "If a patient has hysterical blindness, we naturally assume there is something that he unconsciously does not wish to see, or that his conscience forbids him to look at." (1973, p. 14). The symptom is therefore the observable expression of an unconscious motive, which is unknown to the conscious mind.

These five examples of the existence and influence of unconscious forces on the conscious part of mind show that the unconscious has a dimension wholly different from conscious experience and logical thinking. If this region of the mind is quite unlike our conscious, rational mind, then what does it contain and why are its contents separated from the conscious mind?

The contents of the unconscious, says Langs, "can be terrifying and painful for the conscious mind to acknowledge. They cannot be experienced—reported on—consciously" (1988, p. 30). Consequently, the unconscious deals with thoughts and feelings that would cause great emotional distress if the individual were to be aware of them. It contains impulses, feelings, and thoughts that are often regarded as our dark side.

We can now speak of the mind as consisting of two distinct systems, the conscious and the unconscious. When we deal with an emotionally loaded situation, both systems operate in parallel according to their own ways of experiencing and understanding the meaning of that situation (Langs, 1988). The conscious system's reaction, says Langs, is as follows:

> Something happens to upset us; we react directly, we feel a certain way, we remember certain things, we handle it in a particular fashion. In so doing we are activating what I have called the conscious system and its intelligence, memory storage capacity and the like. And once we have more or less settled the situation, we drop it and go on to other matters. (p. 29)

At the same time the unconscious system is also reacting to the emotional situation. Here, again, is Langs' lucid description of its characteristics:

> Information and meaning...that is too unbearable for direct registration and awareness or has been perceived subliminally is not received by the conscious system. But such information does not evaporate or disappear. These meanings are received by the deep unconscious system, where they are fully and accurately perceived and worked over. The deep unconscious system has its own logic and premises [called primary process], and some of them are difficult for the conscious mind to appreciate. (p. 29)

We can now see how enormously complex the human mind truly is. Every experience with any emotional impact is experienced at a conscious and an unconscious level. The conscious response is logical and problem solving. The unconscious reaction has all those frightening desires and painful thoughts and feelings that the conscious mind finds too distressing to acknowledge, much less to deal with.

PSYCHIC CONFLICT

The thoughts, feelings, and impulses in the unconscious mind are dangerous to the conscious mind. The conscious mind seeks to protect itself by keeping them in "quarantine" in the unconscious. The quarantine, however, is never without some cost and is never totally effective. We pay a high price for trying to keep these thoughts and feelings from our awareness in the forms of restricted self-understanding, creativity, and emotional experience. We must ward off parts of who we are in order to keep these bad thoughts and feelings confined to our unconscious mind. Despite our attempts they still impact on our conscious experience through dreams and symptoms that cause us real distress. It is as if the unconscious wants to tell the conscious mind that there is much important emotional information available, but the conscious wants none of it because it is too painful or frightening to accept.

The result is that the conscious system must refuse potentially valuable emotional understanding of events because it is too frightened of those feelings and the thoughts that go with them. This struggle between the unconscious mind's desire to express thoughts, feelings, and actions that the conscious mind cannot acknowledge forms another fundamental principle of the psychodynamic approach: behavior is the result of conflict between the conscious and the unconscious systems. Our behavior is the product of the unconscious mind's attempts to express and gratify its desires and the conscious mind's defenses against those attempts.

THE STRUCTURAL THEORY OF MIND

Freud (1923) devised a theory of mind to describe the relationship between the conscious, the unconscious, and the individual's development of a system of moral values. He devised a model of the mind that had three components: the id, the ego, and the superego. The id, ego, and superego have their own spheres of influence, but are also influenced by each other. Hall and Lindzey (1957) describe these three parts of the mind this way: "In a very general way, the id may be thought of as the biological component of personality, the ego as the psychological component, and the superego as the social component" (p. 36).

The Id

The first component is the id. The id is entirely unconscious and operates according to the nonlogical principles mentioned earlier by Langs (1988). One important aspect of the id is that it is governed by the pleasure principle. "Its drives always seek immediate gratification or immediate discharge, without regard to the consequences other than the attainment of pleasure" (Cameron, 1963, p. 152). In other words, the id is only concerned with getting what it wants and has no awareness of or regard for the consequences of getting what it wants.

The id pursues pleasure by using the nonlogical, impulse-driven principles that Freud labeled "primary process." It is a mode of mental functioning in which logic plays no role at all. As Cameron says of primary process,

> It includes throughout life the primitive rock-bottom activities, the striving and strange unconscious maneuvers of the human being. It includes (1) prelogical archaic symbolism, (2) a peculiar interchange of expressive vehicles, (3) a tendency to condense the [emotional energy] of many drives into one, and (4) an absence of such logical necessities as negation, resolution of contradiction,

and the recognition of time and spatial relations. (1963,
p. 155)

Let us take a look at each of the four qualities of the id
described by Cameron. The term "archaic symbolism" means
that the symbols used by primary process are far more primitive than the symbols of language and problem solving. They
are much more like the symbols of infants and very young
children before they acquire language and the capacity to use
reason consistently.

The "peculiar interchange of expressive vehicles" refers
to the ability of the id to transfer the energy of a drive from
one process to another should the first one be unable to obtain
satisfaction. So, if a desire seeks gratification by one means
and is blocked, it simply chooses another means that may be
more successful, no matter what that means may be. For example, if an adolescent male seeks sexual gratification but is
blocked, he seeks to relieve his sexual frustration by getting
in a fight. The id switches from sex to aggressive behavior
when the outlet for sexual gratification is blocked because primary process can "interchange expressive vehicles."

The condensing of emotional energy of several drives
into one is a more sophisticated version of switching expressive vehicles. In this case several desires seek gratification
through one outlet. A person's behavior may be caused by
several unconscious motives that latch onto that behavior because it is an available outlet to pursue gratification. Consequently, any single action may be the result of several
unconscious wishes seeking expression and fulfillment
through that action. The lack of negation means the id can
entertain all possibilities—nothing is impossible. Pigs can fly,
hell can freeze over, as long as the id wants it to be so.

The absence of unresolved contradictions, like the lack of
negation, means that the id can maintain opposite feelings
side by side without having to confront the incongruity of the
situation. Feelings of love and hate toward a person may exist
simultaneously in the id without any problem, as could desires to preserve and destroy coexist without having any in-

fluence on each other. The characteristic of primary process to permit opposite desires to exist without confrontation is important because it explains the phenomenon of ambivalence: the simultaneous experience of opposite emotions. The role of ambivalence in police work is the primary focus of this book, so it will be discussed in more detail in this chapter and throughout the book.

The Ego

The second component of the mind in Freud's structural theory is the ego. Its function is to deal with reality, and it operates according to the reality principle that makes the ego "capable of organizing experience and behavior in ways that are rational, precise, practical and appropriate to the human environment" (Cameron, 1963, p. 166). In following the reality principle, the ego organizes perceptions, emotions, thoughts, and actions to cope with both the external environment and the individual's psychological needs. In addition, the ego can also organize abstract ideas into coherent systems. The essential function of the ego is to master the environment and the id (Brenner, 1973). Its job is to make sure that neither external forces from the environment nor internal demands from the id jeopardize the person's ability to survive. The ego must also placate the strict moral rules of the superego without being overwhelmed by them, just as it tries to give the id a reasonable amount of satisfaction without being dominated by its pleasure-seeking demands. In short, the ego is the manager of the individual's psychological organization, trying to make sure that the person has some fun while doing the right thing in a safe environment. It is certainly a difficult balancing act.

The mental process by which the ego carries out its functions is called secondary process. The characteristics of secondary process are "...taking into account the realistic demands of the situation, the consequences of gratification and discharge, the overriding need to protect the integrity of the psychodynamic system, and the opportunities to relieve id and superego pressures" (Cameron, 1963, p. 167).

While the id is entirely unconscious, the ego has conscious, preconscious, and unconscious systems. The conscious system deals with the experience of the immediate present. The preconscious ego is composed of memory, which is not in one's immediate conscious thought, but can be made conscious at will. The unconscious part of the ego "deals with sexual and aggressive urges originating in the id" (Blum, 1966, p. 5). Thus the ego must maintain its reality orientation by controlling the demands of the id's impulses, and it does so by using defense mechanisms. The defense mechanisms will be discussed later in this chapter and in Chapter 5.

The Superego

The third component of mind in Freud's structural theory is the superego. Cameron (1963) defines the superego as "an organization of mental systems whose major functions are those of scanning ego activities at all levels, of supplying approval and disapproval, self-criticism and self-esteem" (p. 188). The superego carries out its monitoring of the ego by applying ethical and moral rules that the child acquires from his or her parents and internalizes so that they become his or her own. These internalized moral and ethical rules are the conscious component of the superego, which we commonly call the conscience. One is aware of conscience by virtue of having moral and ethical prohibitions, but it also operates at the unconscious level as well.

People often report feeling guilty over some thought or act that appears to be quite benign. They do not feel guilty because they have said, thought, or done something that violates the conscious part of their superego. They feel guilty because their unconscious superego tells them they are bad, no matter what they say, think, or do. The unconscious superego never lets up from telling the individual he or she is bad. Just as the id is always pursuing pleasure without considering reality, the unconscious superego is always attempting to instill guilt without any regard for the reality of the individual's thoughts or actions. Consequently, a person may feel guilty either for violating the reality-oriented prohibitions of the conscious part of his or her superego, the conscience, and also for being subjected to the harsh, unreasonable criticism of the unconscious part of the superego.

Besides conscience and its unconscious harsh counterpart, the superego also contains what has been called the ego ideal. The ego ideal is the "positive, nonpunitive side of the superego, involved in the setting of goals and aspirations" (Blum, 1966, p. 6).

THE EGO IDEAL

There has been much debate among theoreticians as to whether the ego ideal is part of the superego or is a separate agency of the mind (Chasseguet-Smirgel, 1985). For the sake of clarity and simplicity, we will speak of the ego ideal as part of the superego.

The ego ideal is basically a view of one's self as perfect and loved. It is an unconscious image of being without flaw or weaknesses and contains

> the ideas of perfection towards which an individual strives in his life; to be a good lover, a good parent, a capable workman, a loyal friend, a considerate neighbor, a responsible citizen, to be honest, to be kind, etc. (Hanly, 1984, p. 254).

The ego strives to attain these perfect qualities regardless of whether or not they can be realized. In this way, the ego ideal represents the goal-setting functions of the superego as opposed to its prohibitive functions located in conscience and its unconscious counterpart (Hanly, 1984). The ego ideal is thus the positive side of the superego in that it sees the individual as capable of being perfect and loved, while the conscience sees him or her as uncontrollable and immoral unless constantly scrutinized and restrained.

Piers and Singer (1971) describe four characteristics of the ego ideal that are particularly relevant to the psychodynamics of the policeman. First, they suggest that at the center of the ego ideal is a feeling of omnipotence, which is required for self-esteem. While too much of this feeling results in setting grandiose ideals,

> a minimum of primitive omnipotence seems to be necessary to establish such healthy, integrative functions as self-confidence, hope, and trust in others. Possibly it also requires a minimum of magic belief in one's invulnerability and immortality to make for physical courage and to help counteract realistic fear of injury and death. (1971, p. 26).

Thus some degree of belief in one's omnipotence and invulnerability to harm is necessary for self-confidence and trust in others. One of the major points of this book is that police work provides the opportunity for the officer to feel all-powerful and invulnerable by mastering danger and is therefore a major source of pleasure.

The second characteristic of the ego ideal described by Piers and Singer is that it "represents the sum of positive identifications with parents" (1971, p. 26). The ego ideal represents the individual's positive images of his or her parents as caring, powerful, and lovable, and these images motivate the child to be like them. Since the role of the police officer is to serve as society's caring, strong and admirable parent, it is possible that young men seek to become officers because the job permits them to take on the positive images of their own parents.

The third characteristic of the ego ideal is that it contains identifications from the individual's later experiences. In addition to positive parental images, the ego ideal also contains positive images of one's peer group. Consequently, the person's reference group also sets standards to be met through his or her internalizing positive images of peers. For the police officer, the peer group is a principal source of perfectionistic ideals to be achieved in order to receive its love and respect. There are specific ideal qualities required to be a "cop's cop."

The fourth characteristic of the ego ideal, according to Piers and Singer, is that it includes the goals of the "mastery principle." This concept refers to "the pleasure of experience in one's own well-functioning." (1971, p. 28). The individual strives to achieve the feeling of satisfaction derived from doing things well. The policeman sees the job as a source of this "pleasure of mastery" when he solves problems or handles dangerous situations.

The ego ideal is a major influence on one's self-esteem. Satisfying the ego ideal brings about pleasurable feelings of self-confidence and self-worth. Failure to attain the goals and images of the ego ideal causes feelings of shame (Piers and Singer, 1971).

CONFLICT AND ANXIETY

The ego, as was said, tries to satisfy the id and the superego while seeking to maintain some control over them. When the ego fails to satisfy his or her conscience by permitting too much gratification to the id, the result is that the person experiences guilt. When the ego fails to live up to the expectations of the ego ideal, feelings of shame are the result. Thus guilt occurs when the ego permits a rule to be broken, while shame results when the ego fails to reach a goal or match an internalized image (Piers & Singer, 1971). When the ego anticipates impending shame or guilt, or being overwhelmed by strong id impulses, it experiences anxiety.

When the demands of the id or superego become so strong that they threaten to overwhelm the ego, the result is that the ego experiences anxiety. Several types of anxiety can be described according to the source of the threat, whether from the environment, the id, or the superego.

The first type of anxiety is objective anxiety. In this type the source of danger is the external environment. The experience of being overwhelmed by danger and feeling helpless is called traumatic anxiety. The ego copes with objective anxiety by anticipating the danger and "taking steps to ward it off before it becomes traumatic. This ability consists of being able to recognize a very slight feeling of apprehension as the signal for something which will become more dangerous unless it is stopped" (Hall, 1979, p. 64). When the danger cannot be warded off, the person experiences trauma.

The second type of anxiety is called instinctual anxiety (A. Freud, 1966). Here the source of anxiety is the id with its impulses demanding immediate gratification. If these impulses become so intense so as to threaten the ego's control, then anxiety is the result. The individual worries that he or she will not be able to control impulses that should not be released from restraint.

The third type of anxiety is superego or moral anxiety. In this case, the superego demands that the ego restrain an id impulse that the ego does not consider dangerous, or the ego ideal expects the ego to meet performance standards beyond its ability. In the former, the ego anticipates feeling guilt for not obeying the superego, while in the latter it anticipates feeling shame for failing the ego ideal.

The fourth type of anxiety does not have a label, but its source is the id (A. Freud, 1966). One of the previously described characteristics of the id is the "absence of unresolved contradictions," meaning the id can contain opposing wishes, side by side, without conflict. Not only can the id maintain these opposing impulses, it can demand that the ego satisfy both of them at the same time. The demand to satisfy conflicting impulses simultaneously causes the ego to experience anxiety because it cannot possibly perform such a task. This type of anxiety plays an important role in the experience of ambivalence, of which more will be said later in this chapter.

How does the ego defend itself from experiencing anxiety? When it is capable of meeting the threat and controlling it, the ego uses its secondary process to find realistic measures to neutralize or reduce the threat, thereby removing the feeling of anxiety. When the threat is perceived by the ego as too powerful to control, however, the anxiety cannot be eliminated by attempting to master the threat.

When the ego perceives a threat from the external environment as too strong to master, as in the case of objective anxiety, it uses fight or flight reactions to avoid feeling overwhelmed. The person simply attacks the threat or runs away from it. In those instances when the ego regards a threat from the id or superego as too strong to control by realistic means, however, it cannot do anything to stop experiencing anxiety.

Since it cannot take any action to end the feeling of anxiety, the ego tries to do the next best thing. When the ego cannot remove anxiety, it utilizes defense mechanisms to avoid experiencing anxiety. This is the psychodynamic version of the old saying, "If you can't do anything about it, try to pretend it isn't there."

DEFENSE MECHANISMS

The use of defense mechanisms allows the ego to remain unaware of experiencing anxiety. Consequently, the ego uses defense mechanisms to avoid feeling anxious when it cannot remove the cause of the anxiety. While there may seem to be nothing particularly wrong with the notion that if you cannot get rid of the problem, then do not let it make you anxious, the ego's use of defense mechanisms does have a price. The cost to the ego is that defense mechanisms "deny, falsify, or distort reality" (Hall & Lindzey, 1957, p. 49).

In effect, the ego must pay for using defense mechanisms by being less able to use its most important asset: the reality principle. The use of defense mechanisms requires the ego to surrender some of its capacity to accurately perceive reality and take reality-oriented steps to deal with internal and external threats. When we use defense mechanisms, our ability to perceive what is really happening and to take appropriate action is weakened.

Although the number of defense mechanisms is potentially endless, there are specific mechanisms that are included on nearly every list. These defense mechanisms will be described in some detail because they will be used in later chapters to explain how police officers deal unconsciously with the anxiety created by powerful id and superego impulses.

Repression

The first mechanism is repression, which is "a defensive reaction by means of which the individual's own painful or dangerous thoughts are excluded from his consciousness without his awareness of what is happening" (Coleman, 1964, p. 99). Repression is involved in almost all the other mechanisms since they all rely on excluding threatening thoughts from awareness. In a sense, repression is the source of the other mechanisms in that all defense mechanisms are based on repression. An example of repression is the inability of the victims of violent crimes to remember any details of the incident or to describe the attacker. The victim cannot remember because the experience is too painful, so the ego unconsciously defends against the potential painful recall by making the memory unavailable to the victim's awareness.

Denial

Denial is the second defense mechanism. It is simply the process of ignoring or refusing to acknowledge painful realities. "We turn away," says Coleman, "from unpleasant sights, we refuse to discuss unpleasant topics, we ignore or deny criticism, we refuse to face many of our real problems" (1964, p. 97). For example, the police officer who reports having no feelings of pain for victims or revulsion at a particularly gruesome crime scene is unconsciously relying on denial to ward off feelings of pain for the victim and helplessness to do anything to alleviate the victim's suffering.

Rationalization

The third defense mechanism is rationalization, which "involves thinking up logical, socially approved reasons for our past, present or proposed behavior...Rationalization has two major defensive values: it helps us to justify what we do and what we believe, and it aids us in softening the disappointment connected with unattainable goals" (Coleman, 1964, p. 98).

The policeman who tells himself that it is all right to accept weekly payoffs from merchants because they are grateful and would be offended if he refused their "gift" is unconsciously using rationalization as a way to defend himself from feelings of guilt for accepting gratuities.

Isolation

Another important defense mechanism used by the ego to ward off pain and anxiety is isolation. The emotional part of one's experience is cut off from the perceptual part, so that one is conscious of a bad experience without being aware of the bad feelings that go with it. Unlike denial, which trivializes both the experience and the emotions that go with it, isolation permits the individual to be aware that the experience is bad but unaware of the pain or anxiety that the experience provokes. Isolation permits the person to emotionally withdraw from a painful situation while consciously and behaviorally remaining in it. An example of isolation is the matter-of-fact manner in which a police officer may talk about a tragic incident. He may acknowledge the tragedy without being aware of his own painful reaction to it; he may say it was terrible without feeling terrible about it.

Projection

Projection is a defense mechanism that is called "dumping" in everyday language. It involves transferring "blame for our own shortcomings, mistakes, and misdeeds to others, and [attributing] to others our own unacceptable impulses, thoughts and desires" (Coleman, 1964, p. 99). The officer who feels powerless to deal with the misery he sees may project this feeling onto the civilians around him so that he consciously feels powerful and regards the civilians, not himself, as powerless. The overly aggressive policeman may project his own hostile impulses onto civilians in order to believe his hostility is merely a reaction to those around him. As a result, the hostile officer perceives hostility coming from everyone else but not from within himself.

Reaction Formation

Another defense mechanism that tries to keep unacceptable impulses and wishes from consciousness is reaction formation. Like projection, reaction formation is a more elaborate defense in which the unacceptable impulses are repressed and the person is aware only of opposite feelings and attitudes. The police officer who feels pleasurable excitement being in the street despite the misery surrounding him may feel anxious because good people are not supposed to feel pleasure from bad situations. Consequently, he may repress the pleasurable feelings and permit himself to be aware only of feeling terrible about being in the street.

Identification

When feelings of anger toward or fear of separation from a loved one become threatening, the ego may use identification as a defense. The person using identification keeps separation anxiety and anger toward a loved one from conscious awareness by modeling him- or herself according to the characteristics of that loved one (Cameron, 1963, p. 236). For example, the police officer who feels anger toward brother officers for demanding that he behave according to their rules may ward off the anger and fear of ostracism by adopting the behavior and attitudes of fellow officers as his own. Thus he consciously experiences himself as being just like his peers, while feelings of anger toward them and of fear of losing them remain unconscious.

Although the weakness of defense mechanisms may make them appear to be used by people who cannot cope with their external and internal conflicts, they are relied on by everyone, not just the emotionally disturbed. We all rely on defense mechanisms because in the last analysis life is too hard for any of us to cope with. Being alive seems to require us to be subjected to powerful feelings of anxiety and other painful emotions that are too strong for us to be aware of during our waking lives. We all need to distort reality in order to cope with it.

The bottom line is that there are no psychological supermen or superwomen, just people trying to deal with the difficulties of their emotional lives as best they can. Consequently, defense mechanisms are not signs of pathology unless they are used to excess; they are, for want of a better term, "normal," because everyone relies on them. In discussing the psychodynamics of police work, I am describing the police officer's attempts to cope with the anxiety and emotional pain of the work as essentially normal defense mechanisms except in those cases where reliance on them becomes extreme.

AMBIVALENCE

As mentioned earlier, one characteristic of the id is that it permits opposing impulses and feelings to coexist alongside each other and to demand that each be gratified at the same time. Holder (1975) notes that the ego cannot tolerate the simultaneous presence of incompatible wishes, ideas, or feelings in relation to someone or something. These opposing wishes, ideas, and feelings undermine the ego's attempt to maintain a balance among them. The term "ambivalence" is used to describe the simultaneous experience of feelings of love and hate for someone or something. Ambivalence is defined as the simultaneous existence of opposite feelings, attitudes, and tendencies directed toward another person, thing, or situation. In this most general sense, ambivalence is universal and not significant because there are very few affectionate relationships which are not uncomplicated by some hostility, and many hostile relationships are tempered by affection. When, however, the strength of these conflicting feelings increases to the point where action seems unavoidable yet unacceptable, some defensive maneuver takes place which often leads directly to mental illness. Under these circumstances, the ambivalence is repressed, that is, only one of the two sets of feelings is permitted to become conscious. Usually it is the hostility which is repressed, but sometimes it is the affection. (Moore & Fine, 1968, p. 19)

This definition is long because the nature of ambivalence is complex. First of all, in ambivalence there are opposing feelings operating at the same time. Second, ambivalence is present to some degree in every emotional experience. The old saying, "It's a thin line between love and hate," is very accurate when the presence of ambivalence is taken into account. Third, when the opposing feelings grow in intensity so that they can no longer be controlled by the ego, repression is used to keep one of the opposing feelings from awareness while allowing the other to become conscious. Fourth, it is usually the negative feeling that is repressed and the positive feeling that is given access to consciousness.

The primary focus of this book is on the impact of ambivalence on police officers and how they cope with it. Policemen must cope with ambivalence from the public, the police department itself, family and friends, and from other policemen. In addition, they must deal with their own ambivalent feelings toward these very same groups.

Finally, the officers must contend with their ambivalent feelings toward the work itself. The street is a source of simultaneous feelings of misery and pleasure for the police officer. How he defends against intense feelings of love and hate for the work is the most important and most difficult psychological adjustment he must make, particularly when repressing one feeling or the other has significant emotional consequences for him, his family, his peers, the department, and the public.

In Chapter 2 we will look at how the policeman experiences being the object of ambivalence. When one is subjected to simultaneous feelings of love and hate from others, it is no less anxiety provoking than having the ambivalent feelings. The officer's own ambivalent feelings toward others is described in Chapter 3, while Chapter 4 explores the feelings of love and hate for the work itself.

The defenses used to cope with either being subjected to ambivalence or feeling it directly is the focus of Chapter 5. The reader may need to refer back to the terms described in this chapter as he or she progresses through the book. I have tried to keep the use of jargon to a minimum, but have not been wholly successful. For this I apologize in advance.

Chapter 2

Why Everybody Loves and Hates Cops

Virtually from the day he enters the police academy, the police officer is the target of ambivalence from just about everyone. He is confronted with ambivalent messages from the public, the police department itself, from his family and friends, and from fellow officers. As described in Chapter 1, ambivalence is the simultaneous feelings of love and hate. The symptoms of ambivalence take the form of "mixed" or "double" messages sent by the ambivalent person to the object of these ambivalent feelings. For example, the police officer may receive feelings of admiration and contempt, affection and hostility, love and hate, from the same individual at almost the same time.

Coping with these mixed messages is difficult enough, but the police officer's problem is compounded by the fact that the ambivalent person is largely unaware of his or her mixed feeling toward the police officer. The ambivalence is unconscious. In fact most ambivalent people would deny having positive *and* negative feeling toward the policeman; they would be conscious of only positive or negative feelings.

AMBIVALENCE FROM THE PUBLIC

It is safe to say that almost all law-abiding Americans have ambivalent feelings toward the police. While historical and cultural factors such as distrust of strong government and a belief in rugged individualism have contributed to our mixed emotions toward the police, there is an important psychodynamic factor that causes the public's ambivalence. Basically, the individual citizen's mixed feelings stem from his or her unconscious reaction to the officer's power to protect or punish the citizen, power the citizen does not have (Westley, 1970; Bittner, 1975). It is the police officer's power to protect and punish the citizen that is the catalyst for the citizen's love and hate of the police officer. Perhaps Niederhoffer says it best:

> The cop is a walking Rorschach in uniform as he patrols his beat. His occupational accoutrements—shield, nightstick, gun and ticketbook—clothe him in a mantle of symbolism that stimulates fantasy and projection.... To people in trouble, he is a savior. In another metamorphosis, the patrolman becomes a fierce ogre that mothers conjure up to frighten their disobedient youngsters. At one moment the policeman is a hero, the next a monster. (1967, p. 1)

What is the origin of the citizen's feeling of love and hate for the police officer? How can he be both savior and ogre? The answer lies in the citizen's unconscious fantasy of the cop as a parent who either provides feelings of safety and nurturance or who inflicts unjust punishment on an innocent child.

The police officer who protects the citizen when he or she is good and punishes the citizen for being bad represents, at an unconscious level, the citizen's parent, and the citizen then experiences him—or herself once again as a child (Menninger, 1965). So, while the individual may consciously perceive the police officer as the arm of the law, unconsciously the police officer is emotionally regarded as parent. Parents, after all, have the power to make the child feel loved and secure when he or she is good and unloved and fearful when he or she is bad. In essence, the police officer's power, and the citizen's lack of it, recreate the citizen's childhood feelings of love and admiration for the loving parent and of hate and fear of the punitive parent.

Anyone who has ever requested help from the police knows how much gratitude and relief is felt when a police officer arrives. At that moment he really does seem larger than life, an all-powerful hero rushing to our rescue. Police officers have often remarked that people appear almost childlike in their admiration for the cop who responds to their call for help. We may well assume that this childlike behavior is based on childlike feelings that have been recreated by the person who feels frightened and unable to handle the situation without a powerful helper.

ILLUSTRATION

An executive, who thought of herself as at best neutral to the police, was riding the subway when she and other passengers were accosted by a gang of teenagers who assaulted some passengers and menaced the rest. When the train doors opened at the next station, a policeman entered the subway car. She found herself running to him and holding him as a child would clutch a parent. She later thought that at that moment she was no longer a woman but a little girl, and the policeman was no longer a civil servant to whom she was indifferent but her "daddy" who would save her from bad people.

On the other hand, anyone who has ever been issued a summons by a police officer knows the feeling of anger at being singled out from everyone else and unfairly punished. The feeling that we are being subjected to the cop's whim or desire to subject only us to his persecution while letting really *bad* people go unpunished is a rather typical emotional reaction of the recipient of a traffic ticket or summons.

ILLUSTRATION

> Officer J. was a young officer attached to the highway
> unit. One day he stopped a car for speeding and discov-
> ered the driver was an apparently wealthy businessman
> old enough to be his grandfather. To Officer J.'s surprise,
> the businessman began whining like a child, complaining
> that Officer J. knew he wasn't speeding and was just
> abusing him to meet the quota for issuing traffic tickets.
> Officer J.'s attempt to calm the motorist by explaining
> that radar had detected him speeding only made him
> whine even more. Finally, the motorist promised never
> to speed again if Officer J. let him go. "At that minute,"
> Officer J. recounted, "I felt like I was old enough to be
> *his* grandfather. After that I expected every driver to be-
> have like a kid when I pulled him over."

McDowell (1975) uses the vocabulary of transactional analysis to describe how civilians unconsciously assume the role
of "victim" and manipulate the police officer into taking the
role of "persecutor." If the police officer allows himself to be
manipulated by becoming punitive, the victimized civilian
then feels justified for hating the officer.

For our purposes, if we substitute the terms "punished
child" for "victim" and "bad parent" for "persecutor," we can
observe how the civilian is recreating his or her experience as
a child being unfairly punished by his or her parent. McDowell points out that individuals are given roles and their corre-
sponding scripts "early in their lives by their parents or other
significant authority figures" (p. 34). Conversely, the civilian
in need of a police officer may unconsciously assume the role
of "good child" and regard the police officer as "omnipotent parent" who will make everything right again. As in the
"victim-persecutor" script, the citizen is largely unconscious of recreating childhood emotions toward his or her
nurturing parent.

Consequently, the police officer arouses childlike feelings
of love and admiration when he is perceived as protecting
and nurturing and feelings of hate and fear when he is perceived as indifferent or punitive. Evidence for this love-hate

experience of police can be seen in the stereotypical good parent or bad parent roles given to police in the movies and on television. The police hero is given what seems to be superhuman strength, intelligence, courage and deductive skills. As one officer put it: "Too many shows show the cop as superman" (Arcuri, 1977, p. 241).

Arcuri's study of police officers' assessment of television cop shows indicated that police felt these shows caused the public to expect too much from police officers. I believe this opinion puts the cart before the horse. These unrealistic expectations have existed in the viewers' unconscious since childhood. Television cop shows did not create them. The appeal of these shows is that they allow us to consciously see what we unconsciously want to believe: good cops are omnipotent, loving parents who protect us because we are good.

However, there are also an ample number of shows that portray the police officer as sadistic, stupid, or both (Culver, 1978). Arcuri's data suggest that police see the "private eye" shows as creating the exact opposite impression in the public's mind from the "superman" cop shows. The private eye shows make the police appear stupid. The private eye, a civilian, has all the brains, strength, and investigative skills, while the police are unable to solve anything. Often they threaten the private eye because he is making them look bad.

Again, I believe those shows in which the police officer is a "malevolent incompetent" do not create an image of the police in the public's mind as much as they reinforce the unconscious image that has been there since early childhood, namely, the cop as the punitive, unloving parent. The stupid, sadistic cop is a fixture in film and television because he allows us to feel justified in hating him. In this case, we identify with his innocent victims. Feeling justified hatred for the sadistic cop has its origin in the viewer's unconscious childhood feeling of hate toward his or her parents for being punitive instead of loving.

These feelings of love and hate exist side by side in the civilian's unconscious mind. When the civilian consciously feels love for the cop, it does not take much to make him or her feel hate if the cop fails to live up to the fantasy of powerful, loving parent.

ILLUSTRATION

> Officer D. worked as an emergency medical response specialist in a suburban police department. He received a call of a heart attack and was the first to arrive at the scene. The victim was already near death, but his wife exclaimed with joy and relief that the policeman had arrived and everything would be all right. Despite Officer D.'s efforts to revive him, the victim died at the scene. At that point, the victim's wife attacked Officer D., shouting that he had killed her husband.

A less dramatic but no less difficult experience for the police officer is the domestic dispute. Typically the woman sees the policeman as her protection from her man but then attacks the officer when he threatens the man with arrest. The following example indicates how quickly and easily love turns to hate:

> Officer N. responded to a domestic dispute to find the woman bruised and bleeding and the man in a drunken stupor. The woman demanded that he lock up her man. Officer N. awakened the man, who woke up swinging at him. While wrestling with the drunken man, Officer N. suddenly felt something heavy on his back and an arm around his neck. It was the beaten woman who had just demanded that he lock up the offender. She had attacked him in defense of her man. Officer N. wound up locking up both of them.

Similar types of incidents occur when a police officer responds to a call from a victim of a crime. Initially the victim greets the officer with warmth and admiration because he or she unconsciously believes the officer will immediately find and arrest the criminal, thus making the victim safe again. However, as the victim realizes that the police officer is not jumping in his car and racing off to catch the criminal, he or she begins to view the officer as *not wanting* to catch the criminal. The victim emotionally perceives the officer as cruelly deciding to let the criminal get away.

A study by Homant, Kennedy, and Fleming (1984) quantifies the victim's view of the cop as malevolent rather than incompetent. They found that burglary victims had a more negative attitude toward police than did a matched control group of nonvictims. Subjects completed an adjective checklist which was scored according to three subscales called Bad Cop, Good Cop, and Helpless. Victims scored significantly higher on the Bad Cop subscale. It is important to note that this subscale contained the following adjectives: cruel, careless, unfair, rash, indifferent, and cynical. The important factor in this study is that victims viewed police not as helpless, but as bad. The inability of the police to protect them caused them not to regard police as impotent, but as cruel. This perception, I believe, is due to the primary ambivalence all citizens feel toward police. Police are admired as omnipotent protective parents until they fail; then they become cruel, punitive parents.

While incidents of love turning to hate are more numerous, it is also possible to convert conscious feelings of hate for the cop to love. Any policeman who has let a motorist go with a warning instead of a summons has observed this sudden transformation of attitude from anger to gratitude. Similarly, a policeman with good interpersonal skills, a good "bullshitter" in police jargon, knows a soft tone of voice or some conciliatory words can turn an angry civilian into a cooperative one.

The public's ambivalence creates a considerable amount of stress for the police officer because he must deal with the citizen's reacting to his or her unconscious image of the officer as a good or bad parent. In these situations the citizen is distorting the true identity of the police officer. The officer's power is legal, not parental. As a result, the police officer is treated as a larger-than-life figure based on the citizen's fantasied past instead of the realistic present. The bottom line is that the officer is in a bind. To the law-abiding citizen who needs him, the officer must be all-powerful and all-loving. To the law-abiding citizen who commits a violation, the officer is an unloving persecutor.

AMBIVALENCE FROM THE POLICE DEPARTMENT

An unexpected source of ambivalence toward the police officer comes from the police department itself. From the day he enters the academy as a recruit, the police officer receives mixed messages from the department. On one hand he is continually reminded that he is part of the cream of the crop of applicants, that he is expected to perform his duties with utmost professional skill, that his personal life must be exemplary, and that his judgment must be excellent since he will be solving problems on his own. At graduation the new cop hears that he has gone through rigorous training that has prepared him to handle any difficulty.

Once he is in the street, the rookie cop usually gets a very different set of messages from the department. He is told that he does not know enough about being a police officer to be left unsupervised for even a brief period, and that his judgment and courage are suspect until he proves otherwise. During this time he also recognizes that the department has a very specific attitude toward him as an individual. Almost all police departments are organized according to the military model of command structure. According to this model, the department's organization is in the shape of a pyramid. The model's basic assumption is that power and knowledge increase as you go from the base of the pyramid to the top.

The department makes it clear to the cop that he is on the bottom, which means that he is expected to follow orders without hesitation and to keep his ideas and opinions to himself (Bennett *et al.*, 1974). In addition, he realized that the department does not regard him as an individual with particular personal attributes, but as virtually identical to all other officers at his rank. It is fair to say that he is viewed as a clone of the prototypical police officer created by the department. Consequently, the cop is interchangeable with all other cops— he has no distinct identity of his own.

ILLUSTRATION

Officer K. was a member of an elite tactical unit. He had recently received his Bachelor's degree in criminal justice and felt he was now a professional in law enforcement. One night his sergeant gave him a detail that involved telling motorists not to park their cars in front of a popular disco. Realizing that being in an elite unit and having a college degree meant nothing to the department's view of him and his abilities, that he was just a faceless employee, Officer K. put in his papers.

The department's ambivalence, like the public's ambivalence, creates stress for the officers because it distorts their identity. Given the department's high expectations of the officers, they are bound to fail because they cannot meet all of them all the time. Police work presents a large number of possibilities for making mistakes, and the officer is bound to make a wrong decision from time to time (Muir, 1977).

Any mistake an officer makes is enough for the department to react with hostility and punishment for failing to be perfect. Conversely, anything that is done well is regarded as unexceptional: the officer is expected to do everything well.

ILLUSTRATION

Officer B. assisted a motorist whose car had broken down. He called for a tow and waited with the driver until the tow truck arrived. The motorist was very grateful and wrote a highly complimentary letter to the police department which commended Officer B. for his kindness and assistance. The department sent the motorist a reply that said that while the motorist's compliments were appreciated, Officer B.'s conduct was no more than was expected of *all* members of the department. Needless to say, Officer B. received no commendation as a result of the letter.

Another example of the department's expectations being a source of stress is offered by Kroes (1985). He describes the impact of being injured in the line of duty as a significant stressor for the cop:

> Put simply, an individual is hurt on the job and is perceived by administration to be malingering and is treated accordingly. Despite his quite real pain, he then also has to contend with a negative reaction from his superiors. This situation is a stressor in and of itself and has come to be known as adding insult to injury. (1985, p. 82)

Here, the department's expectation is that the cop is attempting to collect his salary without having to work for it. In short, the cop is viewed as a potential fraud who is trying to cheat the department.

While being held to superhuman standards of performance, the officer is simultaneously being told that he is to do only what he is told, that his opinions do not matter, and that he requires supervision to perform his duties adequately. Quite a contrast! Thus he is either a Superman or a mindless subordinate. In fact, the police officer is neither, so that these extremely distorted views created by the department's ambivalence are a genuine emotional hazard.

AMBIVALENCE FROM FAMILY

Perhaps the most difficult external source of ambivalence with which the police officer must cope comes from his wife and children. The police wife is proud of her husband for a number of reasons. First, she believes her husband is a member of a noble profession whose duty is to protect society. Second, some of her husband's special status is conferred to her. For example, a police wife is usually not issued a traffic summons when she reveals that her husband is a police officer—a sort of professional courtesy. In addition, her husband may discuss a sensational case with her and disclose details that are known only to the police. Consequently she may feel more knowledgeable about the case by virtue of her husband's special position. It is not hard to see that her role brings the police wife some important psychological "perks" that may make her feel special.

At a deeper, more unconscious level of experience, the police wife may feel more feminine than other women because her husband has a strong aura of masculinity about him. Because other women may see him as larger than life, the wife must be a "real woman" since she is his chosen woman. We get a hint of this feeling from Webber's (1974) description of her feeling toward her husband:

> In no other profession can you feel so much pride and respect for your man. As you see him going about his duties every day, a very warm feeling develops toward him. He becomes your knight in shining armor. This feeling alone compensates for any inconvenience the job may cause. (p. 44)

If he is a knight in shining armor, we may assume she is his fair lady to whom he devotes himself above all others.

The negative impact of being a police wife stems from three sources. First, she may feel that her behavior and that of her children are more closely scrutinized by the community and held to a perfectionistic standard of conduct (Stenmark *et al.*, 1982). Second, the police wife may feel like an outsider when it comes to her husband's work. Although she may be privy to certain inside information about police matters, she feels that he excludes her from knowing what he really does. The typical police officer tries to follow the "leave the job at the station" philosophy when it comes to discussing his work with his family. We will speculate about the underlying motives for this philosophy in Chapter 5, but the impact of this approach is to make the police wife feel like an outsider when it comes to her husband's working life. Furthermore, she may feel that not bringing the job home is connected with her husband's hiding his feelings, particularly his feelings for her (Hageman, 1977).

Closely connected to the police wife's feelings of being excluded is her concern that her husband's work is more gratifying to him than she is. A frequently expressed complaint is that her husband prefers to work than to be with her. The popular expression among police wives, "My husband has a mistress—the police department," conveys the feeling of not being able to compete with the job in providing gratification to her husband. Webber (1974) gives the most eloquent description of the police wife's worry:

> Does your husband spend extra hours at the station? You bet he does. Once police work gets into a man's blood, it becomes his first love and you soon wish it *were* another woman with whom you could at least compete. He eats, sleeps and talks nothing but his job.... Soon you find yourself jealous, feeling unloved (even though he tells you often enough that he loves you) and very emotional and distraught. (1974, p. 22)

My impression is that many police wives dedicate a great deal of effort to keeping their weight down and looking attractive to keep their husbands at home. They explain their efforts in terms of combating the seductions of women whom their husbands encounter while on the job. While this explanation is certainly valid, it seems to be incomplete. I believe these police wives are competing with other women *and* the sexual excitement generated by police work itself. Consequently, the police wife has strongly ambivalent feelings toward her husband—admiration and emotional gratification on one hand, hostility and feeling rejected on the other.

ILLUSTRATION

> Officer G. worked in a suburban department. His wife of two years said she wanted to be closer to him while he was working, so she bought a radio with a police band to listen to his department's communication. At first she felt happy and excited hearing the dispatcher call his car's number for a run. It felt to her as if she were responding with him. However, when he received a call of an armed robbery in progress she became highly

anxious and tearful from fear that he would be wounded
or killed. She waited in panic for his radio transmission
saying he was all right. When he came home after his
tour and saw his wife in panic, Officer G. told his wife
he thought it would be best if she put the radio away.
She refused, saying she wanted to be a part of his work
life, and this was her only way to do it. Her alternating
pleasure and panic continued.

The police officer's child may also have ambivalent feelings toward him. On the positive side, the child looks to his
or her father with great admiration. Clearly the child cannot
help but feel the winner in contests with other kids about
whose father is stronger and braver. The cop's child certainly
enjoys having a special father, one who does all those fantastic
things cops do on television and in the movies.

However, as the child grows older and becomes more
concerned with being the same as his or her peers, having a
cop for a father may cause feelings of estrangement from
friends. In this case the child's special status now turns to
feelings of alienation, of being "different." Consequently, the
preadolescent may begin to resent being singled out from others because his or her father now is no longer viewed as a
hero but as a hostile authority figure.

During adolescence the child of a police officer may feel
particularly isolated from peers since the business of teenagers
is rebelling against authority. Webber's daughter conveys this
dilemma quite well:

> During the period [when you're small] kids find out your
> father is a cop and you're something special.... When
> you enter junior high school the attitude changes and
> sometimes you get roughed up because your dad's a
> cop.... When you're in high school it really hurts seeing
> people hate your father just because he wears a certain
> uniform. (Webber, 1974, p. 39)

The teenager may resent his or her father because his
work has made his child different and therefore suspect. A
cop's adolescent son or daughter may feel singled out as "the

good one" because his or her father is a cop. Adults ought to be able to remember adolescence as a time when "being good" was equated with still being a child who lacks the courage to stand up to adult authority. Times have not changed. Consequently, the cop's teenager feels internal pressure to demonstrate that he or she is just like everyone else and is not more obedient because the old man is a cop.

Those who successfully resist this pressure have opted to maintain their conscious feeling of love and admiration for their father while acknowledging the resentment they feel toward him for making them different from their friends. Those who yield to the internal pressure to prove they are not "good" may be more unruly and hostile to their father than the average teenager because they must repress and deny the same strong feelings of admiration they felt for him during childhood. The cop's teenager therefore may be the most disobedient one in the class or the one getting arrested most often because of the need to prove his or her allegiance to peers. This allegiance requires repressing admiration while permitting only feelings of resentment toward his or her father.

AMBIVALENCE FROM FRIENDS

One of the most frequently reported occupational hazards of police work is that the officer's friends treat him differently once he joins the department. Even as a recruit he finds some friends are reassessing their relationship with him because he is no longer the friend they knew—he has become a cop. Once sworn in, he may be told he cannot be invited to parties because some guests may do drugs there and the host does not want them to risk being arrested by the police officer. Another common experience is having friends refer to the cop in the *past* tense: "You *were* a nice guy, but now that you're a cop I don't know how I feel about you."

Those friends who continue to maintain their relationship with the police officer also express ambivalent feelings toward him. At social gatherings they may get him to tell "war stories" about shootings and other dangerous encounters he has had. This request reflects the feelings of admiration and hero worship felt by civilians, which are the positive side of their ambivalent feelings toward the cop. He may also be asked by the same people to explain why they received a summons when they were not speeding, or he may be told that they know for a fact that cops take graft. These comments are really accusations of the police officer himself and reflect the hostility they feel toward him because of his special power.

ILLUSTRATION

> Officer G. would be invited to parties at which many professional people were guests. When these doctors, lawyers, etc. heard that Officer G. was a policeman, all they wanted to talk about were his experiences in the street. They would almost invariably ask if he ever shot someone or had been shot. When he replied that he had never been involved in a shooting, they appeared disappointed. Their opinion of what a cop is was based on their heroic fantasies of him. After going through this for several years, Officer G. began telling party guests that he "worked for the city" rather than identifying himself as a policeman.

Faced with the risk of being treated like Superman or a corrupt bully at social occasions, many police officers decide not to go to parties. They begin to withdraw from civilian friends and to socialize only with other police officers. We will discuss this issue further in Chapter 3.

AMBIVALENCE FROM OTHER POLICE OFFICERS

When a man joins the police department, he is literally joining a fraternity. In many ways his recruit training in the police academy is as much an initiation into the police fraternity as it is the learning of police procedures and self-defense. The recruit is socialized through "hazing" to begin to talk, act and think like a police officer while shedding his self-concept as a civilian. This new identity as a police officer has strict rules and regulations concerning his behavior on and off duty. It is not merely coincidence that graduation from the academy and receiving a shield is called "being made," the same term as that used to describe inducting pledges into a fraternity and giving them the fraternity's pin to wear.

The socialization process begins in the academy where the police recruit hears two frequently repeated themes. The first is that he must learn to distance himself from the civilian population (Harris, 1973; Van Maanen, 1973, 1975; Burgin, 1974; Gilsenen, 1974). While the inferences of the researchers are that the importance of separating one's self from the public originates in the police culture's preoccupation with danger, another explanation is also plausible. The need to separate from the public may be necessary not only because of the potential danger of unknown members of the civilian population, but also because the police officer is superior to the public.

He has more authority, power, and freedom of action than any civilian. It is he whose job it is to control situations by controlling the behavior of people. In my experience, the theme of the police officer's superiority is communicated in a subtle fashion, but its power is at least as strong as the more explicit message that the public is dangerous.

The second major theme repeated in the academy is that the recruit and future officer must regard his peers as the most trustworthy and dependable people he can have for support. No one else is as reliable as one's brother officers. Consequently, one's fellow recruits become the most important reference group for support and self-identity. As with the theme of superiority, the theme of peer solidarity is transmitted in a subtle style.

As he progresses through the academy, the recruit begins to believe that the police department cannot be relied on or trusted for support. In fact the recruit begins to view the department as he does the public, with a degree of contempt. I believe that one's peers become the primary reference group over the department as a result of the kinds of powerful messages transmitted by instructors and experienced police officers, messages that say the department is the cop's adversary and that the cop has only one group of real friends—other cops.

Once the recruit graduates and joins the fraternity, he is made to feel he is part of an extremely close group of men who are committed to each other. This fraternity shares experiences that no other group of individuals can understand, much less share. The cliché, "brother officer," is a phrase that accurately expresses the importance of the police officer's peers to him and their influence on his behavior and emotions. Studies of the role of peer pressure in shaping the individual officer's attitudes and behavior have stressed the negative aspects of the job, namely isolation, negative public image, and danger as the primary reasons for police solidarity (Van Maanen, 1975; Walker, 1975; Hadar, 1976; Solomon, 1979).

I think it is important to bear in mind that being a member of the police fraternity is also a highly gratifying emotional experience in which the officer sees himself as belonging to an exclusive group of men who are braver, smarter, stronger and more self-reliant than the civilian population they serve. As one of Wambaugh's police officers says:

> Pretty soon you won't be able to feel the same way about your friends in the lodge or church or neighborhood because they won't measure up to policemen in these ways. You'll be able to come up with a quick solution for *any* kind of strange situation because you have to do it every day, and you'll get mad as hell at your friends if they can't. (1970, .p. 81)

By virtue of his membership in this fraternity, the police officer feels he is someone very special. This powerful emotional factor is also a reason for the significant influence of the police officer's peers.

The police fraternity is not confined to members of one's own department. It extends to police officers just about everywhere in the country. Perhaps the most vivid example of this sense of "brothers in blue" is the police funeral. It is common for police officers from departments throughout the country to attend the funeral of a police officer killed in the line of duty. The entire police community shares the loss because it is the fraternity's loss.

On the other hand, the police officer is also subjected to what can only be described as hostility by these same "brothers in blue." One of the most stringent unwritten rules of the police subculture has to do with how a cop is to behave among his peers. The cardinal rule is that a cop must present himself to other officers as a tough, aggressive man of action (Stotland & Berberich, 1979). An incredible amount of a policeman's locker-room behavior is designed to let other cops know how fearless and aggressive he can be. The purpose of this demonstration is twofold. First, the policeman lets everyone know he can be relied on to back up his fellow officers in violent situations. His loud, profane speech says he is not afraid to be aggressive with anyone, cops included. The second purpose of the demonstration is to show that he is a man who will act first and think later. Should he show signs of any emotion except aggressiveness, he may be viewed with suspicion. His brother officers may view him as too weak to be counted on when a dangerous situation develops.

ILLUSTRATION

Officer Y. came home from work to discover that his wife, with whom he had been quarreling, had suddenly left him and taken all their possessions with her. The next day when he reported to work, he sat in front of his locker and began to cry. After a few minutes he recovered and put on his uniform. An officer observed him crying and reported it to the sergeant. The sergeant asked Officer Y. if he was all right. Officer Y. described what had happened the previous day, said he was depressed, but that he wanted to go on patrol rather than go home to an empty house. The sergeant reported their discussion to the commanding officer who took away Officer Y.'s weapon and shield, told him to go on sick leave, and ordered him to undergo a departmental psychiatric ex-

amination. The department psychiatrist examined him
and concluded that Officer Y.'s depression was appropriate given his circumstances and that he should return to
duty. When he came back to work all the officers on his
tour refused to be his partner, saying they couldn't trust
him after he broke down. Subsequently Officer Y. was
transferred to a different precinct.

Why must a policeman have to show his peers that he
can act aggressively and quickly? The answer has a lot to do
with the police culture's basic distrust of cops who "think."
The word "think" in this context does not mean intelligent. It
means reflective. A thinking police officer is regarded as someone who may not act swiftly and decisively, and therefore
may lack confidence in himself, his courage, and his skills. I
have frequently observed police officers in training sessions
receive sarcastic reactions from fellow officers after having
said they had read about a theoretical issue or had devised a
theory about the nature of human behavior. The sarcasm may
have a good-natured quality to it, but it also has an unmis-
takably sharp rebuke in it: "You sound too soft." The message
is clear: the police officer who does not conform to the behavior his peers expect of him risks hostility, at the least, and
ostracism should he deviate too far for too long. Niederhoffer
puts it this way:

> From the insensitive standpoint of the peer group it
> is...the deviant nonauthoritarian individual who is the
> failure. Because he does not inspire confidence in his col-
> leagues and his superiors, he often is relegated to the
> quiet posts or to jobs that do not require active police
> work. (1967, p. 130)

It would seem that the policeman's fellow officers regard
him with ambivalence as do the public, his family, and the
police department. He is awarded membership in a tightly
knit fraternity that is closed to outsiders. In this fraternity he
finds an intense feeling of camaraderie, concern, and security.
It is with his peers that he experiences himself as being understood and accepted because they know what he is going

through. However, his peers also view him with suspicion should he not continually act as a tough, decisive, profane man who acts rather than "thinks." Being soft, reflective, and anxious are definitely not permitted in the company of other officers.

Since virtually every human being is going to feel soft, reflective, and certainly anxious on occasion, the subculture is in effect hostile to these qualities in the policeman and demands that he get rid of them. Consequently, even the cop's peers are a source of stress because they are also ambivalent toward him. Although they regard him with care and provide him with intimacy and understanding that no one else gives, they also regard his inherent "noncop" qualities with hostility and require him to hide them.

To sum up, the police officer endures stress because just about everyone, police and civilians, family and strangers, has ambivalent feelings toward him. They have the strongest positive emotions for him because he is the public's omnipotent parent, his family's knight in shining armor, the department's highly skilled professional, and his peers' brother officer. Simultaneously, he is also the public's malevolent, inadequate parent, his family's withdrawn and depriving husband and father, the department's mindless subordinate, and his peers' undependable coward.

As one can imagine, the amount of stress the police officer experiences as a result of being the object of ambivalence from all quarters is considerable. However, it is by no means the only or even the major source of stress he must grapple with. In addition to contending with being the *object* of ambivalent feelings from everyone, he also has to cope with *his own* ambivalent feelings toward everyone else—the public, the family, the department, and his peers. We will explore the police officer's own ambivalent feelings and the stress they create in Chapter 3.

Chapter 3

Why Cops Love and Hate Everybody

Coping with people and social institutions who express both love and hate for you at the same time is a difficult job. For the police officer, however, this task is only a part of the complex and difficult job of dealing with both the ambivalence of others and also *his own* ambivalent feelings toward them. The police officer's problem is that he is not simply the *object* of ambivalent feelings from the public, the department, his family, and fellow police officers. He has comparable feelings of love and hate for them as well.

It is not easy for anyone to be the object of love and hate, but it is certainly more difficult to come to grips with one's own ambivalent feelings for others, especially when the individual is not completely aware of them. We are all more objective and more able to keep our emotions in check when we are dealing with other people's conflicts than with our own. In this sense, the police officer's job of coping with the ambivalence of others is less stressful than managing his own feelings of love and hate for them. Resolving the problems of being loved and hated by the public, the department, and one's family and peers is much easier than recognizing and living with one's own love and hate for them.

AMBIVALENCE TOWARD THE PUBLIC

Cops have a real love–hate feeling for the public. On one hand, cops want the public to recognize their importance and to admire them for being brave and skillful. It is a common occurrence when police officers are interviewed on television news programs to say they want the public to recognize that they are doing the best they can to make the streets safer, that they want to be seen as helpers rather than as enemies, and that their job would be much easier if the public would be aware that cops are as human as everyone else. These statements are a litany of clichés, but they are clichés because the police genuinely believe them. The police officer really does want the public to love him because he views the citizenry as an important source of personal gratification. Public recognition and admiration are as important to the police officer as they are to everyone else, perhaps even more so.

The man who chooses police work as a career does so in part because being a cop satisfies his vocational needs and his personal need to be recognized as valuable and meaningful (Preiss & Ehrlich, 1966; Symonds, 1972). Van Maanen's (1977) field study of the police academy experience found that recruits chose police work because they saw it as meaningful. He found meaningful work to be a more important motivation than job security or money, noting,

> security and salary aspects of the police job have been overrated. [Instead] a rather pervasive meaningful work theme is apparent as a major factor in job choice. Virtually all the recruits alluded to the opportunity afforded by the police career to perform a role which was perceived as consequential or important to society. (1977, p. 295)

Symonds (1972) describes a primary motive to choose police work as "recognition hunger." Using the analogy of the school monitor to explain this motive, Symonds says the school monitor craves recognition from adults and seeks to imitate authority figures to receive approval. In addition to the need for recognition, Symonds suggests police officers also have a corollary "need to be liked," which causes them to choose police work.

I believe that the "need to be liked" is more accurately described as the need for approval from authority, not by peers, and that a different need, one for admiration from the general population, also exists for the police candidate. Consequently, the police officer's need for recognition is complex; it comprises the need for approval from the police department and the need to be admired by the public.

Public recognition of his valuable role is an important source of gratification of the officer's need for admiration, and the clichés on television news are a direct expression of that need. When the public fails to satisfy this need, the officer expresses his unhappiness clearly and unequivocally (Niederhoffer, 1967; Lefkowitz, 1974; Van Maanen, 1975; Buzawa, 1979). The officer's personal need for recognition and admiration from the public is accentuated by the police department. Through formal training in the academy, the department explicitly tells the future officer that his function is to serve the civilian population, and that his ability to get along well with the public will be evaluated by the department.

In addition, commendations and administrative rewards are given to those officers who receive complimentary letters from grateful citizens while punishment awaits those who get letters of complaint from unhappy civilians. As a result, the cop sees the public not only as an important source of gratification for his need to be recognized and admired, but also as a vehicle for approval and reward from the police department. That, to put it mildly, is a great deal of emotional clout the public exerts on the police officer.

On the other hand, police officers also view the public in exactly the opposite emotional light. Along with seeing the public as important in gratifying their need for admiration, cops also feel the public is contemptible at best and dangerous at worst. They regard civilians who ask for assistance as being too weak or lazy to take care of themselves or as potential assailants (Skolnick, 1973). So it is a rare police officer who does not develop what he believes is a healthy and wise wariness toward the public, because the citizen is a source of only distress and danger, not of satisfaction.

Where does the officer's strong hostility toward the public come from? I think it comes from the same sources as his positive feelings, namely, his own personal need for admiration and the police department's accentuating that need. The officer's need for recognition and admiration from the public is a complicated affair. My guess is that embedded in the term "need for admiration" is the fantasy of hero worship. We may often admire a person without regarding him or her as superior to us, but as an equal with special qualities or skills. However, we may also admire someone for being heroic—braver, stronger, more skillful than we are. We view this heroic individual as our superior rather than our equal. Many police candidates are seeking admiration as heroes, the kind that says he is braver, stronger, and better than more ordinary men.

In fact, one of the police academy's first tasks is to disabuse the new recruit of his fantasy that police work is essentially nonstop acts of bravery and strength that are beyond the capacity of the average citizen. My impression is that this fantasy persists at an unconscious level despite the academy's attempts, despite the everyday routine of police work once the officer is working in the street, and despite his conscious acceptance of the fact that his job is more mundane than heroic. His power and authority, even when handling routine calls, give him a sense of superiority over civilians that is emotionally quite gratifying and is manifested as a conscious feeling of condescension toward the citizenry.

Ironically, the second source of the officer's hostility toward the public is the police department, the very institution that says the police officer must serve the public. While the department's *formal* instruction emphasizes how important the public is to the future police officer, academy instructors and training officers *informally* teach the recruit to have a very different attitude toward the public. This informal instruction can be labeled "the street cop's view of the public," and it says, as Van Maanen (1977) aptly puts it, that the public

> is comprised exhaustively of three types of citizens. These ideal types are (1) "suspicious persons"—those whom the police have reason to believe may have committed a serious offense; (2) "assholes"—those who do not accept the police definition of the situation; and (3) "know-nothings"—those who are not either of the first two categories but are not police and therefore, according to police, cannot know what the police are about.... The "know-nothing" may be the injured or wronged party or the seeker of banal information and as such is treated with a certain amount of deference and due respect by patrolmen. (p. 223, p. 224)

The last sentence of this quotation uses the phrase "deference and due respect." However, a more accurate term may be "tolerance." The officer tolerates the average law-abiding citizen because he is a victim or a supplicant, but he does not respect the relatively powerless and needy citizen. As many police officers have described it, the experiences of assisting civilians is more akin to a feeling of benevolent superiority in that the powerful, capable police officer renders help to the powerless, inferior civilian. Niederhoffer's view of the policeman's feeling of superiority is that he

> has the power to regulate the life of others, a role symbolized by his distinctive weapons and uniform; likewise his constant dealing with crime may encourage him to view policemen as superior to the general race of men. (1967, p. 92)

So what has happened to the civilians whose recognition and admiration is so important to the cop? The street cop's view of the public says they do not exist. The public, says the street cop's view, is his inferior—less knowledgeable, less self-reliant, less powerful. As a result, he is less likely to be respectful in encounters with civilians (Sykes & Clark, 1974).

It is the officer's experience of his own greater power in contrast to the relative powerlessness of civilians that causes his feelings of hostility and contempt for the public. Repetitive encounters with people needing his help or rebelling against his greater power reinforce the cop's feeling of superiority over civilians (Niederhoffer, 1967).

ILLUSTRATION

> When he first came on the job, much of Officer R.'s time was spent issuing traffic citations. At first he was polite, as he had been taught to be, but after a year of hearing unbelievable excuses, threats, and thinly veiled bribe offers, Officer R. came to see motorists as stupid, or liars, or both. Soon he stopped trying to hide his contempt and began asking violators for their special license for the handicapped since they had to be blind or mentally retarded to have driven so badly.

These polar opposite attitudes toward the public, namely, the need for recognition and admiration versus hostility and condescension, exist side by side unconsciously in the police officer. Consciously he may be aware of only one of these attitudes, depending upon the situation. Before the television camera he may truly want the public to appreciate and admire him. On patrol he may truly feel all the people around him are "suspicious," "assholes," or "know-nothings." Both feelings are real for the police officer, but he has trouble consciously recognizing that both feelings exist. I might add that allowing one's self to be aware of opposite emotions gives everyone trouble, not just the police officer. Recognition and resolution of ambivalent feelings is one of the most difficult aspects of gaining self-awareness for everyone.

Perhaps the police officer's ambivalence toward the public is a hidden factor in Buzawa's (1979) observation that

> most officers have contradictory perceptions of their occupation. On the one hand, they perceive policing as having low status in the community [not enough recognition and admiration]. On the other hand, most studies show that there is a strong belief that the occupation is indeed very valuable [superiority]. (1979, p. 94)

Buzawa goes on to speculate about the impact of the disparity between low prestige from the community and high self-esteem derived from police work, and she suggests that one possible result may be the "garrison mentality," a combination of a tightly knit police subculture and a hostile attitude toward the general public (1979, p. 94).

I think the "garrison mentality" is a group manifestation of the individual police officer's attempt to cope with his ambivalent feeling toward the public. The police officer does not want to be cut off from the public; he wants instead to be held aloft on the public's shoulders as a hero. However, he also feels the public is composed of "know-nothings" who are not his equal. When civilians unconsciously wrestle with their own ambivalent feelings for the police officer by denying the wish for him to be an omnipotent, loving parent and seeing him only as the inadequate, punitive parent, the officer responds by denying his own need for admiration because he unconsciously knows his need will not be gratified. He permits himself to be conscious only of his hostile, contemptuous feelings toward the public, and he then withdraws from the public to his "garrison" of fellow cops.

Every American who has seen two or more Western movies knows that the brave, strong, good guys of the cavalry are inside the fort, while outside the walls are uncivilized, sneaky, primitive, warlike Indians. It is not too much of an exaggeration to say that the police officer's garrison mentality states that the civilized, brave, good guys are on the inside of the station house walls, and those on the outside are the weak, demanding, ungrateful hostile primitives who are the public.

As you can see, the garrison mentality expresses not just hostility toward the public, it also expresses the officer's belief that he is superior to it. This conscious attitude of superiority keeps the officer's need for admiration from the public at an unconscious level, causing him to be aware only of his feelings of hostility.

Another sign of the officer's ambivalence is his mixed feelings toward assisting civilians. Police officers like to get complimentary letters from citizens because they are personally rewarding and enhance their chances for commendation and promotion. However, the term they use to describe being polite and persuasive in assisting individuals or mediating disputes is "bullshitting." The term clearly indicates that behaving in a polite or conciliatory way to civilians is to lie to them. Why is being courteous a deceitful act to the officer? Because every cop knows that the public is not worthy of his respect, so that behaving respectfully is really a disguise of his true feelings. As a result, the cop who gets many complimentary letters is envied because he is getting the recognition and admiration all cops want. Yet at the same time he is called a great bullshitter, an expert liar.

Should a police officer be so conciliatory and polite to civilians that he seems to undermine his superior position over them, his behavior is called "stroking." This term alludes rather obviously to stroking the civilian's penis to provide him sexual gratification. The cop who "strokes" makes the civilian happy but he has sacrificed his authority in the process. In gratifying the civilian, he has renounced his dominant, powerful position and has in effect become sexually subordinate. Quite clearly, this is a cardinal sin in police work.

A policeman who treats the civilian as an equal is actually castrating himself by giving away his position of superiority. His need to be liked has undermined his strength and authority. Furthermore, his peers now view his bravery and strength with suspicion. So it is not surprising to find that most policemen do not mind being polite and helpful to civilians as long as they can explain their helpful behavior as concealing their true feeling of condescension toward an undeserving, ungrateful, and weak public. This "deception" permits the policeman to be helpful without surrendering his superior status in the process.

In a sense, the dilemma of having to choose between stroking or behaving with contempt toward civilians is the basic problem of ambivalence and how to manage it. The police officer's need to be admired by the public conflicts with his feeling superior to the public. As a result, when the police officer speaks out of both sides of his mouth about his feelings for the public, he is not being a hypocrite, but is simply expressing both sides of his ambivalent feelings. The problem is that he does not acknowledge that these opposite feelings exist *at the same time.*

AMBIVALENCE TOWARD THE POLICE DEPARTMENT

The police officer loves and hates the department in much the same way as the civilian loves and hates the officer himself. Just as the civilian feels the policeman is both the all-powerful, nurturing parent and the incompetent, malevolent parent, so, too, the officer feels the same way about the police department. His unconscious emotional experience is that he is the child and the department is either a powerful, nurturing parent or a bungling punishing one. Reiser (1982) describes the officer's unconscious perception of the department in terms of the officer being a child:

> The police department represents a family to individuals working within it. The chief of police is the father figure, with all the consonant feelings related to power, dependency and independence.... The "brass" are usually older, more powerful siblings who behave in a paternal and patronizing way toward the young street patrolmen who occupy the role of younger siblings striving at competing for recognition, acceptance, and adulthood. (p. 125)

In Reiser's metaphor of the department as a family, the policeman seeks approval and reward from the chief who personifies the parental power of the department to nurture and gratify the officer. Unconsciously, he sees the department as invulnerable and omnipotent, believing the department is immune from the pressures and influences of other government agencies and social institutions. Furthermore, the police officer feels that his membership in the police department's "family" allows him to share the department's power and immunity.

This unconscious perception of the department exists across the spectrum of the police rank and file, from recruit to seasoned veteran. Symonds (1972) describes this perception as an attitude of reverence for authority which "demands that superiors always be supermen and always on a pedestal. It is an attitude that can render an individual policeman prone to one of the industrial hazards of police work, namely: disillusionment and cynicism" (p. 168).

This "reverence for authority" and its demands that superiors be omnipotent can be viewed as the product of a powerful unconscious fantasy of the department as omnipotent parent. The recruit seeks membership in the police family because he unconsciously wants the department as idealized parent to protect him, thereby making him invulnerable, and to nurture him by giving him some of its omnipotence so that he, too, may be on a pedestal over those who are not members of the police family.

Images of great strength, bravery, and aggression, along with a fantasy of immunity from anxiety and fear, seem to be bound up in the recruit's unconscious wishes for gratification from police work. These unconscious wishes appear to coexist with accurate conscious expectations of what the job will actually be able to provide him. Despite his conscious disavowals, the recruit is unconsciously caught up in the department as an omnipotent parent who will make him invulnerable to threat and superior to the public. Once the recruit becomes a police officer, powerful feelings of hostility toward the department become evident, but they do not eliminate his equally strong unconscious feelings toward the department as an omnipotent parent. Here, unconscious positive and conscious negative feelings exist simultaneously. More will be said of the negative feeling later on, but for now we will continue to focus on the positive feelings.

The new police officer places great emphasis on receiving commendations and getting promoted. He usually explains his desire for promotion and medals in terms of attaining a higher salary and better working conditions. These explanations are of course, accurate. Sergeants do make more money than policemen, and decorated police officers are usually given some consideration for preferred assignments.

However, I believe there is also significant emotional importance attached to promotion and commendations in addition to money and assignment. When the department gives medals or stripes to the officer, it is also giving him its approval. In effect the omnipotent parent is rewarding him for his behavior and now is regarding him as "special." My opinion is that policemen need to feel the department regards them as special because it nurtures and gives them some of its omnipotent power.

Experienced police officers also have a strong desire for the department's approval despite a conscious hostile attitude toward it. Perhaps the happiest men in police work are 10- or 15-year veterans who are promoted to sergeant. Outwardly hard-bitten and seemingly blasé about their new rank, they nonetheless appear to display the emotional reactions of the recruit who has just been made an officer. When told they look very happy, many of these new sergeants would grudgingly acknowledge some happiness, but they would quickly counter with some sarcastic criticism of the department for taking so long to promote them.

The reader will notice that in speaking of the cop's feelings toward the police department as omnipotent, loving parent, I have not cited any references to the literature. The fact is that I was unable to locate any research studies that obtained data regarding positive feelings of police toward their department. I suspect the absence of such data is due to the officer having relegated positive feelings to his unconscious mind while permitting himself to be aware of only his hostility toward the department. In a sense, the officer consciously views the department as the cop hater views the officer—all malevolence and incompetence—while keeping feelings that he wants the department to be his benevolent and omnipotent parent confined to his unconscious mind.

There are several studies that have detected considerable hostility expressed by policemen toward their department. Their hostility usually results from what they perceive to be particular kinds of failings of the department. First of all, there is the lack of what officers regard as a genuine opportunity for promotion (Preiss & Ehrlich, 1966; Lefkowitz, 1973; Reiser, 1973; Hadar, 1976; Griffen *et al.*, 1978; Fagan & Ayers, 1982). Officers express their dissatisfaction with the department's failure to promote them in terms of its arbitrary and unfair promotional procedures.

The cops see the system promoting people for reasons that have little to do with police work while denying promotions to those who do real police work well. They view the department as capricious and self-serving in promoting those whom it favors rather than those who really deserve a higher rank. Cops often say the department punishes good cops and rewards cops who "play the game" instead of doing a good job. Sparger and Giacopassi (1983) found the three reasons most frequently cited as sources of dissatisfaction were lack of opportunity for promotion in the department, departmental politics, and the feeling that one's efforts were not appreciated by the department. In fact, most of the officers who left the department said the failure to be promoted was their primary reason for resigning. Consequently, the typical police officer sees the department as deliberately depriving him of his deserved reward.

Consciously, the reward is the stripes; unconsciously, it is parental love and approval. As a result, the police officer denies the unconscious wish for love from the omnipotent, nurturing parent while being aware of only the conscious hostile feeling that the department is unfairly punishing him and depriving him of approval. All he is aware of is that the department has revealed itself to be a bad, inept parent rather than the good parent he unconsciously wishes for.

Another of the policeman's frequently expressed criticisms of the department is that it is weak. He sees the department as cowardly in facing up to criticism of the police and to political pressure from city hall (Toch, 1979). Buzawa's (1984) interesting finding was that police officers were less dissatisfied with their own status in the community than with what they felt was the department's low status in the city government. Toch (1965) described anomie in police officers as partly due to their seeing "superiors as removed from street problems, subject to political manipulation, and imprisoned by community concerns" (p. 7). When cops talk to each other about the department, it is almost a litany of examples of the department's ineptitude and its willingness to abandon them to the press, the public, and the politicians to protect itself. The officer's conscious thoughts that the department is weak reflect unconscious feelings that it is a malevolent, incompetent parent who has withheld nurturance and has refused to protect him from harm. A third negative attitude toward the department has to do with its arbitrary and punitive control of its officers. Using a questionnaire based on Maslow's hierarchy of needs, Lefkowitz (1973) surveyed the needs of police officers and obtained an interesting result. Police placed greatest importance on self-actualization and security. They also expressed the feeling of greatest deprivation of their need for self-actualization and autonomy by the department. These data suggest that cops are concerned with achieving all their potential and self-reliance and at the same time they are also concerned with basic protection from physical and financial danger.

On the surface these results are not surprising. Cops want to be the best they can be and they are also concerned with protecting themselves from the dangers inherent in the work.

On a less conscious level, however, these concerns reflect their underlying need for protection and nurturance from the department, and their feeling of deprivation indicates the degree to which the department has failed to gratify their need. The officer wants the department to help him become stronger while providing nurturance and protection, as a good parent should. However, the department's command structure makes the police officer feel insignificant and its disciplinary style makes him feel vulnerable to sudden, arbitrary punishment from a parent. As a result, he comes to fear and hate the department for its indifference to his needs and malevolence toward his welfare. He feels the department is using its power to harm rather than to nurture him. The following story demonstrates the officer's desire for approval from the department and his sense of betrayal when he receives punishment instead.

ILLUSTRATION

While on plainclothes assignment, Officer F. and his partner spotted a drug buy in progress. As they approached the pusher and the buyer, the pusher spotted them and ran to his car to escape. Officer F. stood in front of the car, drew his unauthorized semiautomatic pistol, and ordered the pusher to get out. The pusher reacted by starting the car and trying to run down the officer, who then shot the pusher as he tried to speed away. Officer F. felt that he had performed well and anticipated being written up for a commendation. He was written up, but for carrying an unauthorized weapon and endangering innocent bystanders by firing at a moving vehicle. Incensed at being punished for "bullshit," Officer F. vowed to get revenge against the department by never again taking any risks and doing as little as possible. He said if the department didn't want cops to do police work, he would oblige it by not doing anything except come to work, hide, and go home at the end of his tour.

On many occasions I have heard officers in training sessions say that the purpose of the training was to enable the department to cut itself loose from a cop who might get into trouble. They believed the department could claim the cop failed to use the correct techniques he was taught in training and thus avoid lawsuits. So training was merely a ruse to permit the department to escape liability by blaming the cop rather than supporting him. In these training sessions, some officers would wonder aloud if the classroom had been bugged by the department to catch them saying they do not always follow departmental rules and regulations. These remarks were almost always uttered in a half-joking and half-serious manner.

Consequently, the policeman is beset by a mixture of intense feelings of love and hate for the department, a mixture he rarely consciously acknowledges. More typically, the officer compartmentalizes his mixed feelings so that he feels love for the department as omnipotent loving parent when he is promoted or given commendations, and feels hate for the department as incompetent malevolent parent when it is indifferent to his needs for nurturance and autonomy. By compartmentalizing his feelings so that he does not have to deal with having mixed emotions toward the department, the officer is handling his ambivalence toward the department in much the same way as the civilian handles his or her ambivalence toward him. I believe this similarity in coping styles is due to the same unconscious experience of being the dependent, powerless child who wants his parent's love and protection, but also fears receiving punishment and deprivation instead.

AMBIVALENCE TOWARD FAMILY

Having simultaneous feelings of love and hostility for his family is one of the most complex and problematic experiences the officer must grapple with. While ambivalence toward the public and the police department is handled by compartmentalizing love and hate into conscious and unconscious experiences, this strategy does not work with one's family because love is the only permissible feeling the officer believes he can have. Consequently, hostility must be warded off, usually through the mechanism of denial.

It is common for a police officer to become very concerned, even preoccupied, with his family's physical safety after he has been working in the street. Seeing how easily people can become victims makes him acutely aware of how vulnerable his family is to harm. Often the policeman will place a high priority on moving from the city to a more rural area in the hope that his wife and children will be less likely targets of predatory street criminals. He feels a strong need to protect them since they are precious and fragile in his eyes. With this need to protect them goes a strong sense of obligation to secure their safety, and feelings of guilt occur when he is working nights or overtime instead of being home with the family.

The officer may constantly warn his teenage children of the dangers of being out late, hanging out and not being cautious. When his child counters with the age-old retort "everyone else is doing it," he will describe seeing kids mangled in car accidents, mugged, stabbed or shot to emphasize his warning that these things happen all the time. One officer told me,

> My daughter wanted to go to a rock concert downtown at ten o'clock. I said, "There's no way you're going. Do you want me to show you the bloodstains in front of the theater where you want to go?" These kids don't know what can happen to them, but I do.

Having stated the obvious about the policeman's genuine love and concern for his family, we shall also examine his feelings of frustration and hostility toward his family. As with most men, the police officer has ambivalent feelings toward his wife and children. In the police officer's case, however, these ambivalent feelings may be more intense because of the impact of his job on his emotional life and his relationship.

A cop's ambivalent feelings toward his wife can be detected from the way he may describe his love for her. Police officers speak of their wives in a combination of medieval chivalry and Victorian patriarchy. As Webber described her police officer husband as "my knight in shining armor" (1974, p. 44), so, too, the policeman talks of his wife as his "lady" (Megerson, 1973; Stratton, 1975). If he is her brave, powerful, chivalrous knight, then to him she must be the adoring, fragile lady whose self-concept orbits around him and his achievements.

In addition to seeing his wife as his lady, the cop also sees her as his self-reliant subordinate. He expects her to carry out her responsibilities as homemaker without making demands of him to assist her (Maynard & Maynard, 1982) and to refrain from questioning him about his work or anything connected with his "other life" as a cop.

This Victorian view of the police wife as someone whose tasks are to take care of the house and rear the children without leaning on him and to keep from making inquiries about his job are based, according to Reiser (1978), on

> a strong need of the officer to assert his independence,
> to bolster his male ego, and to be free to come and go
> without feeling tied down or corralled.... His wife is
> expected to keep her own needs and problems to herself,
> to not rock the boat or impose an unnecessary burden
> on her overburdened, hardworking husband. (p. 39)

The emotional difficulty of maintaining an "ordinary" husband's role after being a very special authority figure at work can cause serious consequences for both the officer and his wife. The experience of accepting the far less gratifying role of husband may make the policeman more intolerant at home or unwilling to stay home. The next illustration presents an extreme example of this problem:

ILLUSTRATION

> Officer C. was a very active street cop who was so caught
> up in his work that his sergeant was concerned he would
> take too many chances and get hurt or killed. However,
> Officer C. remained very active, so much so that he found
> himself unable to stay home for any extended period

without feeling suffocated. He took a second job which required him to be on the street and often went to it on his days off just to hang out. He could not help feeling that being home and hearing his wife talk about unimportant family matters was choking him, so he would avoid staying home at all costs.

His contradictory emotional views of his wife, that is, his "lady" versus his "self-reliant subordinate," cause the policeman to have mixed feelings about her. To the extent she is fragile, passive, and adoring, her husband feels like her strong protector. However, if her passivity and fragility cause her to ask him for help, then she becomes a helpless incompetent who cannot manage her responsibilities without assistance. In short, she becomes a civilian—someone whom he wants to admire him, while at the same time an intrusive burden because she needs him to help her.

Conversely, if the policeman's wife accepts her role as self-sufficient homemaker, as Webber (1974) suggests she should, then he will love her for not being a burden on him. But the more independent she is, the less he sees her as his "lady." The more self-reliant she becomes, the less admiration she provides him. There is no hero worship, no gratification of his need to be the strong, brave protector. As a result, she must be fragile without being dependent and self-sufficient without losing her admiration for him as her knight in shining armor. Should his wife carry out her role as self-reliant homemaker too well without continuing to make him feel that he is her "knight," then her husband may react as if he were ignored.

ILLUSTRATION

Officer E.'s wife felt that since he had a satisfying job and expected her to "handle things" at home, she would search for satisfying experiences which were independent of their relationship. She and a friend started a small business which became successful very quickly. With her income nearly matching his police officer's salary, Mrs. E. spent progressively more time out of the house, caus-

ing her husband to feel unimportant to her. He then
started an affair and made no attempt to conceal it from
his wife. When she discovered his affair, his wife sued
for divorce.

The policeman has similar ambivalent feelings toward
his children. He enjoys the hero worship given him by his
adoring children. As mentioned in Chapter 2, the policeman's children are always the winner when they and their
friends compare their fathers in strength and skill. The
officer's kids view him as being more heroic than other fathers because he is a policeman. It is fair to say that the police
officer derives considerable pleasure from this very real form
of hero worship.

When his children approach adolescence and go through
the ritual of challenging parental authority, the officer suffers
a great deal of frustration and resentment in contending with
his children. He feels angry with these demanding, ungrateful,
insolent rebels and sees them as assaulting his position of
power with a kind of malevolence reminiscent of the hostile
civilians he encounters in the street. Frequently police officers
confess that at these times they react to their rebellious children as if they were dealing with assholes in the street.

Being treated as an equal by his self-sufficient wife and
as a hostile authority figure by his children may make the
officer feel that family life makes him feel "ordinary," while
being on the job makes him feel special. My hunch is that
feeling ordinary at home and special at work is largely unconscious, and that most policemen would deny that such an
emotional dichotomy between home and work exists.

If my hunch is correct, then Maynard and Maynard's
(1982) study of stress in police families is both revealing and
meaningful. After administering a questionnaire to 42 policemen and their wives to assess the stresses on the police family
and an inventory to measure the family's coping strategies to
those stresses, they found that over half the wives "indicated
that they get the impression that officers do not think that
marriage and families are important" (p. 310). In addition,

nearly three-fourths of the wives said their husbands feel police work is more important than their marriage and families.

However, the police officers saw themselves as being involved with their families. They did not perceive how important their work was to them, although it was very evident to their wives. Their lack of awareness of how much gratification they received from the job is most likely due to the defense mechanism of denial (Hageman, 1978). Denial permits one to keep anxiety-provoking feelings from consciousness by denying that these feelings exist. It is difficult for any man to consciously be at ease with the feeling that there is an intense gratification he receives from his job that his family cannot ever provide him. This issue will be discussed in greater detail in Chapter 5.

AMBIVALENCE TOWARD OTHER POLICE OFFICERS

One of the more surprising discoveries I made while working with police officers is the considerable ambivalence a cop feels toward his brother officers. Civilians invariably see the public displays of brotherhood among the police—the highly ritualized police funeral at which police officers from distant cities and states are prominently displayed in the mass media, the long lines of cops responding to appeals for blood donations for a wounded policeman, the staunch defense of officers accused of excessive force, and the by now tired metaphor of the "blue wall of silence" concerning protecting police officers suspected of misconduct. We civilians see only the close bond among police officers and the strong sense of fraternity resulting from their shared experiences which are, for the most part, unknown to us.

The typical police officer feels very close to his peers for several reasons. First, he sees them as his only reliable support in the street (Savitz, 1970). Because he regards civilians as being indifferent at best and dangerous at worst, other cops become the policeman's only reliable allies in times of trouble.

Should the cop find himself in danger, he expects civilians to behave as neutral nonbelligerents who will leave the scene or simply watch him struggle without offering to help. Only brother officers can be relied on to come to his aid.

Second, the policeman believes other cops are the only ones who can truly understand his experiences and empathize with him and his attempts to cope with the dilemmas of being a policeman. He derives enormous gratification from his sense of belonging to his select fraternity and comes to define his self-worth in large measure from feeling accepted and supported by fellow officers.

Since his self-concept is intimately connected to his membership in the police fraternity, the worst emotional experience a cop can have is to be ostracized by brother officers. Loss of membership in the fraternity is perceived as being far more painful than departmental punishment. Consequently, his peers have more power to punish him than does the police department because the officer's primary affiliation is with other cops, not with the department.

The policeman's willingness to risk departmental punishment in order to keep his peer group's approval is evident in the following example.

> Officer B. was a driver for a sergeant whose alcoholism was widely known throughout the precinct but was never reported. On one night tour the sergeant showed up for work so drunk that he passed out in the radio car as soon as he and Officer B. went on patrol. Rather than driving the sergeant back to the station house and reporting him unfit for duty, Officer B. threw the sergeant in the back of the radio car and covered him completely with his overcoat. Then Officer B. put on the sergeant's hat, whose gold braid and shield identified *him* as the sergeant, and impersonated the sergeant in responding to calls for a supervisor.

Clearly, Officer B. was more concerned about protecting the sergeant from departmental punishment, and himself from peer group sanctions for giving up another cop, than he was about being punished by the department for impersonating a supervisor.

Many newly promoted sergeants have revealed their anxiety about losing the friendships they have had with their former peers. Even though they sought promotions, they were struggling with a feeling that they had lost a part of their identity that had evolved from being in the street with fellow officers. In fact, their self-identity as street cops was strong enough for a significant percentage of these new sergeants to say that being a supervisor would not alter either their self-identity or their working relationships with their former fellow officers whom they would now supervise. They would always be cops on the inside even though they wore stripes on the outside. This powerful need to hold onto one's self-concept as a police officer often causes a new sergeant to renounce his authority and to behave in the field as if he were a police officer.

This reaction creates obvious administrative problems for the department. One senior police administrator called these supervisors "cops with stripes" instead of sergeants because they were unwilling to leave their self-concept as a cop behind them and to assume a new self-concept as a sergeant. The bond with brother officers provides such intense emotional gratification for the police officer that he is reluctant to let it go, even when he is awarded higher status in the department.

The public almost never thinks of police officers as having hostile feelings for each other. There are, I think, two reasons for this. The first is that the law enforcement community has an overriding need to appear unified to the public. If the police regard themselves as an elite, closed fraternity, then their special status may be threatened should dissension become evident to civilians. The police community believes it must guard against the outside perception that it is vulnerable because such a perception may weaken its social and political power.

The second reason the public does not see hostility between police officers is that individual officers must ward off their negative feelings toward their peers. To express hostility might jeopardize their membership in the police fraternity. In psychological terms, it is dangerous to be angry at the source of one's gratification and support. Consequently, the policeman must deny hostility toward fellow officers in order not to put his membership in the fraternity at risk. As a result, police officers rarely express anger to each other directly, but they rely on sarcasm, practical jokes, and unflattering gossip to express their anger in an indirect fashion.

What are the origins of the policeman's hostility to his peers? First of all there is the pervasive rivalry that begins in the academy and continues throughout his career. Many police departments encourage competition among recruits for best grades by awarding preferred assignments after graduation according to the officer's recruit class rank on tests. Recruits with the highest test average have the best chance of receiving their first choice of precinct location. While there is certainly nothing wrong with this strategy of motivating recruits to do their best, one consequence of this approach is to foster hostility among those recruits who do not excel on exams and performance ratings for those who do.

This atmosphere of competition continues on the job, especially when the date for the sergeant's exam is posted. Once again, the police officer who wants to be promoted engages in direct competition with his peers for the highest score on the test. Frequently the police officer who gets promoted is subjected to resentment and backbiting from his unsuccessful competitors. Newly appointed sergeants often express the worry that friends who are now their subordinates will ostracize them or try to undermine their authority by treating them as peers rather than as supervisors.

Competition is also evident among policemen with respect to "good" arrests. There is an undertone of competition among officers concerning who makes the best and the most "collars." One policeman says, "There's a lot of competition. The real active cops know how many collars the other cops made."

It is not my intention to suggest that rivalry and hostility in police work is qualitatively different from those in other professions. There are many professions in which rivalry and hostility are quite obvious. However, there are no professions that I know of in which very intense feelings of camaraderie, loyalty, friendship, and elitism are mixed with strong feelings of anger and a kind of "everyman for himself" struggle for advancement.

The second source of the police officer's hostility toward other cops stems from his suspiciousness toward them. As with his competitive feelings, the officer's suspicious attitude toward his peers can be seen in the academy where recruits are instructed to stay clear of any cop suspected of being corrupt (Gilsenan, 1974). Recruits are told to be wary of being friendly with other cops until they are sure those cops are not corrupt. Guilt by association is the essential pitfall the recruit is instructed to avoid. As a result, there is again this ambivalent mixture of fierce loyalty and suspicion the individual policeman feels toward his peers. This set of loyalty and suspicion makes the officer both dependent on his peers and predisposed to seeing them as dangerous. The following story highlights the complexity of his feelings and the unhappy consequences they can bring about.

ILLUSTRATION

Officer A. was assigned to a plainclothes unit that was rumored to be under investigation by Internal Affairs for widespread corruption. He received an invitation to lunch from an old friend from his academy days and his first year in the street. When his friend met him at the restaurant for lunch, he was carrying a briefcase that he brought with him to the table. Officer A. became nervous about the briefcase. He confronted his friend about not checking it with his coat and accused him of carrying a "wire" in the briefcase to set him up. The friend said if that's what he believed, then their friendship was over. The friend then opened the briefcase in which there were textbooks—his friend was going to college.

Finally, the third source of hostility toward brother officers, and the most difficult to deal with, is the feeling that the
fraternity itself is a deception. Just as he believes the police
department would readily abandon him in crisis to protect
itself, the cop also feels that he cannot trust all of his fellow
officers to come to his aid if he were in danger. This uncertainty about the reliability of peers is rarely stated explicitly.
Instead, it takes the form of preoccupation with "back up."
The one thing every officer wants to know about another is:
Can I trust him to back me up? We civilians believe that it is
a given that every available officer responds to a policeman's
distress signal. If this were the case, police officers should not
be so concerned about "back up" because it would be so reliable. However, cops do think quite a bit about the reliability
of their peers.

The uncertainty about back up seems predicated on the
worry that the officer cannot trust other cops to come to his
aid. In this regard, a study by Savitz (1970) surveyed police
officers to determine whether assisting another police officer
had highest priority. He found that

> experienced officers are most likely and detectives least
> likely to render aid to an endangered officer regardless
> of setting.... Significant is that in instances of greatest
> peril to a fellow officer, twenty to twenty-seven percent
> of the police subjects would not go to his aid but would
> respond to a recent murder, and over ten percent would
> pursue a child molester. (p. 703)

Consequently, the police officer's suspicion that he cannot always count on brother officers to back him up seems to
be justified. Savitz's study suggests that the officer suspects
he will not get back up if something "more important" is
going on. Furthermore, another set of statistics seems to high-
light the officer's ambivalence toward his peers. Savitz also
found that 95 percent of the rookies (three months in the field)
surveyed said that an officer can always count on back up
from other cops. However, 27 percent of the same group of
rookies also believed that "there are a significant number of

policemen who will try to get out of doing anything to help other officers" (Savitz, 1970, p. 701). This simultaneous expression of opposing feelings is about as clear an example of ambivalence as can be found.

It is this diametrically opposite pair of powerful beliefs about one's peers that contributes much to the individual police officer's ambivalence toward other cops: he can always count on them all the time versus he cannot count on all of them all the time, and on some of them any of the time.

The task of dealing with one's own ambivalence toward others is more complicated and difficult than that of coping with the mixed feelings of others. Grappling with our own mixed feelings is a much tougher assignment than absorbing simultaneous feelings of love and hate from others. However, both of these situations are easier than contending with ambivalence toward an internal reaction to being in the street. In this case, the officer feels love and hate for an experience in which no one else plays a part. There is nobody else involved in the policeman's ambivalence toward the actual experience of doing the work. There is only the officer and his intrapsychic conflicts created by the work itself, which is the main topic of the next chapter.

Chapter 4

Why Cops Love and Hate the Work

HATRED FOR THE WORK

One of the happiest days in a policeman's life is graduation day at the police academy. It is a day filled with emotionally loaded symbolism: the march into the auditorium, the speeches extolling his professional skill, the proud faces of his family members in the audience, and the feeling of a masculine rite of passage in which he is now a member of an elite fraternity of brave and powerful men who protect the weak and defend the virtuous.

In psychodynamic terms, graduation day confirms the young officer's unconscious feeling that he has fulfilled the expectations of his ego ideal. He has become the strongest, the bravest and the most competent of men by having become a policeman. He now eagerly looks forward to demonstrating his omnipotent ability in the street by helping people and protecting them from criminals. For him, the street is an opportunity to experience the realization of his ego ideal.

However, the nearly universal experience of policemen once they hit the street is the staggering amount of misery and degradation that runs rampant there, and the lack of real power they have to do anything about it. The new cop is inundated with suffering and cruelty and can do very little to stop it. One police officer says of his first months on the job:

> My first month on the job was in Harlem. In that first month I pulled three babies out of incinerators. There was such a casual acceptance of violence there. When I went home and drove across the Triborough Bridge, I felt like I was going to a completely different world and would wonder what would happen if these people that I left would also cross the bridge and come into the other world where my family lived.

These experiences of misery and horror, and of the feeling of impotence to stop or prevent them, lead the police officer to two conclusions. The first is that being a cop has destroyed his faith in the dignity of the human race. Human beings are too corrupt, too cruel, too self-degrading to deserve care or protection (Kirkham, 1974). The second conclusion is that his efforts to bring some sense of justice and order to the street are meaningless. No matter how hard he tries to make things better, he will fail because evil and degradation will always defeat him. Eisenberg (1975) describes the cop's encounter with feeling overwhelmed in this way:

> Much of police work generates a sense of uselessness and meaninglessness. Frustrations are profound for those police officers who seriously endorse the value of "helping people," a value which frequently is the first to go with exposure and experience. The inability to effectively function and successfully deal with people's problems confronts the police officer daily. The forms of adjustment are numerous ranging from learning to be satisfied with the few and rare successes to clear and apparent apathy. (p. 32)

In a real sense the cop's experience in the street parallels the G.I.'s experience in Vietnam. Lifton (1973) speaks of the Vietnam vet's being caught up in an all-encompassing absurdity and moral inversion. Tne absurdity has to do with a sense of being alien and profoundly lost, yet at the same time locked into a situation as meaningless and unreal as it is deadly. The moral inversion, eventuating in the sense of evil, has to do not only with the absolute reversal of ethical standards but with its occurrence in absurdity, without inner justification. (p. 37)

For the policeman in the street, the feeling that he is trapped in some absurd, meaningless struggle trying to help people who seem unable or unwilling to help themselves, who subject themselves or others to unspeakable cruelty, and who hate him even though he is there to help leads to a belief that the whole world is, as one of Baker's cops said, "all a sewer" (1986, p. 333).

The officer's feeling that he is stuck in a moral inversion also has a profound impact on him. In this moral inversion what he has come to value as good and right is not only attacked, it is turned upside down. Consequently what he thought were valued beliefs and behaviors are now regarded as harmful to him should he try to live by them in the street. So, kindness and respect for others now becomes bad because civilians are undeserving and cannot be trusted to accept the cop's kindness without trying to use it against him. Conversely, hostility and suspiciousness become good since they help protect the officer from the undeserving, untrustworthy, and dangerous population surrounding him.

Nearly every policeman can tell of an experience in which he tried being kind and paid dearly for it. Here is one of them:

ILLUSTRATION

While patrolling a subway station, Officer H. spotted a homeless woman lighting a cigarette on a staircase. Feeling some pity for her, he told her in polite words that she was not permitted to smoke in the station. She thanked him in equally polite language. As he turned from her and headed downstairs, she pushed him off his feet and he tumbled down the staircase. Bruised and

> stunned but otherwise unhurt, Officer H. raced up the
> stairs, beat the woman senseless, and arrested her.

These nightmarish experiences in which kindness is equated
with putting one's self at risk create in the officer a powerful
belief that if he wants to make it home at the end of his tour,
he must never make the mistake of thinking that people
should be treated well. On the other hand, always remember-
ing that civilians are dangerous and contemptible will help
insure his safety.

In addition to witnessing misery and cruelty and being
unable to stop them, and in believing that the Golden Rule
of behavior has no validity in the street if he is to survive,
the officer also is struck by the painful realization that all his
effort and bravery are meaningless. In the street his presence
and his sacrifices for the well-being of others have no meaning—nothing will change. His second conclusion is that he
is trapped in dangerous yet meaningless attempts to make
things better. This bitter realization causes him to doubt the
meaning of life itself. He suffers from existential anxiety from
which there seems to be no relief.

ILLUSTRATION

> A policeman answered a call for help from a tenement
> building. When he got to the apartment door, he knocked
> and announced his arrival. The door opened a crack, and
> a man stuck a shotgun through the opening and fired a
> blast into the officer's chest, killing him instantly. An of-
> ficer in the same precinct was badly shaken by his death,
> not only because he was a good cop and a good man,
> but also because the way he died was totally senseless.
> There was not a shred of truth to the cliché that he did
> not die in vain. His fellow officer asked, "What was it
> all for? Why should we go out there and get killed if it
> doesn't mean anything? I mean why are we doing this?"

These simple questions were anything but rhetorical. They
were real questions to which neither he nor I could come up
with any appropriate answer. These questions state the
officer's quandary of being immersed in a meaningless yet

dangerous environment in which he feels helpless and from which he cannot escape.

The feeling of uselessness and the sense of being immersed in meaningless suffering is clearly a psychically painful experience, particularly when the officer unconsciously sees the job as a vehicle to satisfy the demands of his ego ideal. In psychodynamic terms, the policeman's feelings of powerlessness and of being trapped in meaningless suffering are terrible blows because they constitute his failure to live up to the expectations of his ego ideal. The omnipotent, heroic person he unconsciously thought he could become on graduation day from the academy has not been achieved. Instead his encounter with abject misery and incredible cruelty in the street, coupled with his feeling powerless to prevent or stop them, cause him consciously to feel a sense of defeat for having failed to be the all-powerful, brave defender of justice he sought to be.

At an unconscious level, the policeman believes he has failed to live up to his ego ideal and feels shame as a result. He unconsciously blames himself for not having been good enough to reach his ego ideal, especially after having come so close by becoming a cop. A veteran police officer said to me that the problem with cops is that they are failed idealists, and that is why they become cynical. Perhaps he is right. But from a psychodynamic perspective, the problem with cops is not that they are failed idealists as much as they are failed "ego idealists."

Now that police work has become a source of shame rather than gratification, the officer comes to hate his job. He hates being a cop. He tells himself that choosing to be a police officer was an enormous mistake, perhaps the greatest mistake of his life, because seeing human beings at their worst and feeling powerless to do anything to make things better have changed him permanently for the worse. Furthermore, his efforts to bring justice to bear are not only futile, they are meaningless.

At this point he becomes preoccupied with worrying that if his sacrifices are meaningless, he, too, will be meaningless.

Many policemen with this preoccupation worry that continued involvement with "human garbage" may infect them psy-
chologically until they too become human garbage. In the
1970s the Patrolmen's Benevolent Association of the New York
City Police Department ran a public relations campaign to encourage the public to be more sympathetic to the police. One
of the more memorable ads was a poster showing a police
officer lying unconscious halfway out of his radio car with
his head near an overturned garbage can. Even though the
poster was designed to elicit sympathy from the public, it conveys an unconscious message that the officer is not only in
danger, but he is also surrounded by garbage.

The metaphor of being surrounded, overwhelmed, and
ultimately tainted by human garbage, and here garbage is itself a metaphor for the cruelty and degradation he sees every
day, is also evident when officers describe themselves as
society's garbage men. They say society hires them to sweep
away the human garbage it does not want to see and that
inevitably the garbage rubs off on them, making them feel
degraded and spiritually sick. Two defense mechanisms used
by individuals to avoid feeling helpless are to lash out at anyone identified as being responsible for creating the frustrating
situation and to withdraw emotionally from the situation and
become detached and seemingly indifferent.

The policeman's hatred for the work and how it makes
him feel is powerful and genuine. It is not a psychological
distortion of his experience. If his hatred for the job is real
and intense, the question must be asked: Why does he stay?
Why does he remain a cop when he truly hates the work?

Kirkham (1974) offers one explanation for the policeman
remaining on the job:

> Why does he stay with it? The only answer is to experi-
> ence a sense of satisfaction over his contribution to soci-
> ety—something I have never known in any other job.
> Somehow that feeling seems to make everything worth-
> while, despite the disrespect, danger and boredom so
> often associated with police responsibility. (p. 136)

Kirkham's explanation for police choosing to stay on when the work is so demoralizing is the "altruism hypothesis." His assumption is that police officers are essentially altruistic, so that the work gratifies their altruistic impulses, which enables them to endure the repulsive aspects of the work.

A very different hypothesis to explain why police officers do not quit the job they hate is presented by Breslin (1973):

> There a number of reasons why a policeman in New York takes a job as a policeman, nearly all of which are the pension. The pension...runs a policeman's life. It is the only thing he is afraid of losing and it is the only thing he wants out of the job.... At the end, he is a terribly bitter old man who wonders if he has wasted his life.

Breslin suggests that it is purely his concern for financial security that keeps a police officer from resigning. This "financial security hypothesis" is supported by many policemen who state loudly and often that the pension is the only reason they are still on the job. One policeman explains,

> I've seen a lot of guys come and go. You know what I've never seen? I've never seen a guy quit.... As soon as you're on the job four or five years and you're making good money, you can't quit. You're a high school graduate and now you're 26 years old. Where are you going to make [as good a salary]? Now what do you do? Got to go to work, but you hate the job. Hate it. Despise it. Most of it is in your head. You just can't get up for the job anymore. (Baker, 1986, p. 344)

The financial security hypothesis assumes that the only gratification in being a police officer is the pay check. So policemen endure the misery and demoralization for the money and for nothing else.

Both these hypotheses are insufficient to explain why policemen do not quit their jobs despite the emotional and spiritual pounding they receive. First of all, the altruism position requires that public service and self-sacrifice are the primary motives for policemen to stay. In my experience, neither of these motives account for an individual's decision to remain

a police officer because police officers do not seek altruistic
self-sacrifice in their work. As Toch (1965) says, "If the [job
were so bad], only saints or madmen would be tempted to
enter the police profession, whereas experience tells us that
most law enforcers cannot be classified under either of these
headings" (p. 22).

Second, the financial security theory assumes that emotional gratification plays no part in policemen choosing to remain in law enforcement. This theory is easily contradicted
simply by listening to retired police officers. If the financial
security theory is correct, after receiving the long-awaited pension the retired cop should be incredibly happy to be away
from the misery of the street. However, my interviews with
retired policemen indicate that they miss the job a great deal,
primarily the feeling of being special. Now that they are civilians, retired cops often feel a sense of loss of self-esteem.
Many show signs of clinical depression connected to that feeling of loss. As one policeman described it,

> You see guys who find it very difficult to retire from the
> P.D. It's become more than a way of life for them. It's all
> those toys, those gifts that he has, that specialness that
> he feels. To give that back and go back to the real world,
> that's what the tremendous surrender is. (Baker, 1986,
> p. 343)

A police officer described his friend who retired this way:

> All he talks about is how he made a real mistake.... He
> misses whatever it was he had out there. Whether it was
> the excitement of the job, whether it was the power, I
> don't know. Some guys, you take the power and distinc-
> tion of being a cop away from them and they're just an-
> other Joe Schmoe looking for a job...it's degrading.
> (Baker, 1986, p. 353)

These quotations indicate that the pension at retirement is far
from the singular gratification provided by police work. It is
obvious that many police officers feel a sense of loss rather
than reward upon retiring and collecting their pension. And

it is just as obvious that they derived an important and intense emotional reward from the job itself.

LOVE FOR THE WORK

If neither altruism nor money can fully explain why a policeman chooses to continue to endure misery on a daily basis, then there must be something more that a policeman gets from the job. There must be a significant emotional reward in the work itself for him to put up with its seamy side. I believe the emotional reward comes from intense feelings of excitement and power, feelings so gratifying that they are, as one policeman told me, "Better than sex."

There are unique aspects of the work that provide the policeman with this "peak experience" of excitement and power (Van Maanen, 1974). The unique aspect that provides intense excitement is the danger inherent in the job. Police work is dangerous in a way that makes it special. The adrenaline rush created by responding to a call or anticipating a suspicious person's behavior is strong and very pleasurable. One officer describes it as "a rush—it's the obvious importance and intensity of the decision [you must make]. It's the moment you feel most alive. It's the decision that could end a life." That rush, that feeling of being completely energized in preparing to deal with danger is sensually invigorating and addictive. Once anyone, policeman or civilian, has that feeling, he or she wants to have it again. The fact is that for most of us this "turn on" is unavailable from our jobs. But police work, particularly working in the street, provides the opportunity on a fairly regular basis, even in low-crime areas.

At first glance the idea that policemen love the job *because* of the danger seems absurd. After all, who would want a job that puts one's well-being at risk? The answer is that everyone has the capacity to be "turned on" by danger, provided he or she chooses to take the risk and master it. When one voluntarily subjects him or herself to danger, there is an exhilarating rush that cannot be replicated in safe conditions. People who play dangerous sports describe their emotional experience as one of intense pleasure. They also describe their emotional reaction to being successful in their attempts as one of great pleasure with themselves.

If the experience of subjecting one's self to danger and emerging victorious in sports is so pleasurable, then perhaps it is not so far fetched to consider that the policeman's emotional reaction to being in the street and successfully handling dangerous or potentially dangerous situations may be very pleasurable in terms of the adrenaline rush of excitement and the self-satisfaction he feels. One police veteran made this observation about the thrill of facing danger:

> There's a big difference between [being] accidentally scared and being voluntarily scared. When you are walking down the street and two guys come out of a liquor store after holding it up, that's accidental danger. I executed a lot of warrants in my career. That moment before you announce your presence and break down the door, you're leaning against the wall with a sledge hammer, you don't know what's behind the door. It could be a guy with a shotgun. And you ask yourself, "Do you really want to do this?" And I always said, "Yes." That's what I call voluntary danger.
>
> The feeling [choosing to be in danger] is exhilaration—the highest form of exhilaration. There is no higher form. The greatest sexual, fearful, and joyful intensity. When you get that high, they're all the same.

There are a few studies that provide indirect support for this hypothesis. For instance, two studies (Teevan & Dolnick, 1973; Griffeth & Cafferty, 1977) administered the Rokeach Value Survey to police officers and found that the need for excitement was rated as a very important value. Orpen (1982) found that job involvement with one's work is greater if the job is physically dangerous. Police officers also showed interest in activities on the Strong Vocational Interest Blank that are categorized as "risky" (Johannson & Flint, 1973). Finally, Skolnick (1973) surveyed police officers to determine which assignments they preferred. He found that 87 percent preferred assignments that were more dangerous, while only 4 percent preferred less dangerous inside jobs. Skolnick concluded that the police officer "may enjoy the possibility of danger, even though he may be fearful of it" (1973, p. 136).

Cullen, Link, Travis, and Lemming (1983) came to a similar conclusion after conducting a survey of police officers' perceptions of danger on the job. They found that police see their job as inherently dangerous, but do not believe they will get hurt because they are alert and ready to master the danger. Lawrence (1978) found that police do not view the danger in the work as a source of stress. They regard stress as a function of the degree of control the officer has over the situation: the more control or mastery he has, the less stress he feels. Finally, police officers report relatively low levels of death anxiety, even though they are in a dangerous profession (Wenz, 1979). This is the essence of the police officer's emotional experience of the work. He is fearful yet pleasurably excited by the danger and intensely gratified in mastering it.

Research has provided only indirect support for the "pleasure in successfully dealing with danger" hypothesis. More direct support comes from two nonscientific but extremely valid sources: Joseph Wambaugh's earlier novels and Mark Baker's *Cops*. In Wambaugh's *The New Centurions* (1970) and *The Blue Knight* (1979), the principal characters are policemen describing their emotions while on patrol.

In *The New Centurions*, a rookie's more experienced partner says, "I can't help stomping down on a 459 call. Love to catch those burglars." Serge's [the rookie] reaction was to be glad "to see his partner's blue eyes shining happily. He hoped the thrills of the job would not wear off too soon on himself" (Wambaugh, 1970, p. 49). This description of the partner's reaction demonstrates both the excitement felt in responding to a call and the pleasure created by that excitement. It is obvious that all crime-in-progress calls are dangerous, but that the dominant emotional response of the policeman is excitement and pleasure as well as fear. Consequently, the stimulation created by fear, the conquering of fear, and mastering of dangerous calls are especially gratifying.

Wambaugh describes the experience of a self-doubting policeman as he goes off duty during the Watts riots of 1964:

> He completed the night as he had begun it, quivering, at moments near panic, but there was a difference: he knew the body would not fail him even if the mind would bolt and run.... The body would remain and function. It was his destiny to endure, and knowing it he would never truly panic. And this, he thought, would be a splendid discovery in any coward's life. (1970, p. 350)

Not only splendid but incredibly pleasurable as well. Experiences such as these provide a special emotional stimulus that is both unique and potent in its gratifying effect on the policeman.

The second ingredient in police work that makes it so gratifying is the experience of real power. There seems to be a potent stimulant in being the authority on the street where the policeman has not only legal but real physical power to control both people's behavior and the outcome of events. He is the omnipotent hero of his ego ideal, capable of protecting the good and the weak from the bad. He has become the man he sought to be on graduation day from the academy. One officer describes his experience as the actualization of his fantasy of being a cowboy hero:

> It's like Dodge City and you're the sheriff. The street is mine and ain't nobody going to fuck with it. That's a great and professional feeling. You've done something, you're important. Up until then in your life you may have done nothing. Now all of a sudden, at the ripe old of age of twenty-one, there's a whole lot of people looking to you to protect them from the madhouse around them. That's a wonderful thing. (Baker, 1986, p. 18).

Power brings a feeling of real importance and superiority that, to say the least, is very pleasurable. Another police officer describes the pleasure of being in the street this way:

> People are paying attention to you. They want to talk to
> you. There's a whole ego trip that goes with the job. You
> start saying to yourself, "Am I special?" They have been
> telling me that I am. (Baker, 1986, p. 18)

The transformation from anonymous civilian to police officer with power, a kind of fame, and a feeling of superiority
have a profound impact on the officer's self-concept. He begins to regard himself as more capable, stronger, and smarter
than the civilians he polices. The job has made him the person
he dreamed of becoming. The job gives the feeling that he is
truly special and superior. It is a feeling that policemen recognize and share among themselves—it is their own secret. I
believe this feeling of being special and superior is one of the
things that binds the police fraternity together.

The psychodynamic description of the experience of mastery of danger, of having real power to make others behave
properly, and of having the ability to make things right is that
it provides a feeling of having achieved the unconscious expectations of his ego ideal. The policeman who feels powerful,
superior, and heroic at these moments is savoring a kind of
pleasure that few people can enjoy—he has met the demands
of his ego ideal. During those pleasurable moments his self-
concept and his ego ideal are the same. He is in fact the powerful hero he unconsciously sought to be. This experience is,
as the insightful officer pointed out earlier, "the highest form
of exhilaration." It is described by athletes as a feeling of physical perfection; but this state is tame in comparison to the
policeman's, who feels not only physical perfection, but also
heroic and powerful as well. What cops share, says one veteran officer, is a feeling of importance:

> You show up and stuff stops happening. It's more than
> a power trip, it's the recognition that your presence
> makes a difference to somebody. Carried out with class
> and dignity, it's sexy—it's like hitting one out of the park.
> I was proud. I knew who I was. You hit a rooftop, you
> take a kid home who is out at 3 o'clock in the morning,
> you keep some asshole from harassing a young girl, you

> get a smile from an old lady because she'll be able to
> cash her social security check with you standing there.
> It's electric—fucking electric.

This sense of being special and powerful that comes with the job cannot be duplicated in any other aspect of the policeman's life.

The policeman's feelings of shame and pleasure for both failing to meet the expectations of his ego ideal while at the same time becoming that ideal pose a difficult emotional paradox for him to resolve. Here is a job that makes him consciously feel overwhelmed by misery and powerless to do anything about it. Here is a job that exposes him on a daily basis to the worst aspects of human nature, forcing him to become cynical in self-defense. At the unconscious level of his experience, the officer hates the job for making him feel shame for failing to live up to his ego ideal.

Yet at the same time here is a job that gives him a strong adrenaline rush in facing danger and mastering it. Here is a job that makes him feel superior because of the power it gives him. Consciously he feels gratified by the work; unconsciously he feels narcissistic pleasure for achieving the goals set by his ego ideal. The ambivalence of hating and loving the job for making him feel both shame and narcissistic pleasure is a difficult emotional conflict to cope with. Yet it is not the only emotional conflict about the work with which he must contend.

In addition to the conflict between shame and pleasure brought about by failing and satisfying his ego ideal, the policeman also faces another powerful unconscious conflict between the raw pleasure provided by the street and his own morality. Besides providing him with the pleasure of meeting the demands of his ego ideal to be brave, virtuous, powerful, and special, the job also gives the officer a more basic pleasure of being the most important, the most powerful, the most admirable man in the street. The job also gives him the feeling of being immune from the social, legal, and moral restraints that restrict the pleasure-seeking behavior of a less powerful and important man. He is, in effect, free to do as he wishes because no one has the authority to challenge him in the street (Niederhoffer, 1967).

The special status to be above the law because he is the law is a source of enormous pleasure, the kind of pleasure that cannot be found in the conventional nine-to-five world of the civilian, the kind of pleasure that satisfies the most basic and primitive needs of every human being. It is the pleasure derived from the exercise of power over others without concern for its consequences. As one of Baker's policemen says,

> Policemen have this sense of "I don't care who you are, you're not a cop." You can be President of the fucking United States of America or a goddamn brain surgeon, but you're not a cop. I'm special. I can give you a summons and you're going to listen to me. I may go home to my above-ground pool and drink my beer, while you're off to drink Dom Perignon someplace. Nevertheless, for that moment in our lives, I'm the boss and you're the shithead. (Baker, 1986, p. 343)

The policeman in the street is the law whom everyone must obey or face punishment, to whom everyone must defer or face punishment. The pleasure of being in charge and having no one to answer to is a very special one, the kind that has often been equated with the rush provided by sexual activity. The problem is that this kind of pleasure is immoral in the eyes of one's conscience. Our moral code tells us we should treat others as we would have them treat us, that we should not exercise power for its own sake but for some higher moral goal, that we should remember that we are all God's children, no matter how much or how little we have. Consequently, the policeman's being turned on by his sense of being immune from restraint in the street collides with his moral code that says that he should reject this pleasure because it is bad.

It is not surprising that policemen describe the street as a prostitute, someone who tempts him with immoral pleasure, someone toward whom he feels both contempt and desire. Wambaugh's characters in *The Blue Knight* (1979) refer to the street as "la puta," the whore. This description of the street as a whore sexualizes the police officer's ambivalent feeling toward the street. He has contempt for the street and also is strongly attracted to it at the same time.

The metaphor of the street as whore also conveys a complication in the policeman's ambivalent feelings toward the work. Since the street is a whore, the good man should not be seduced by it. He should be able to resist its temptations and to reject the gratification it offers. To accept the pleasure of the work means to accept *illicit* pleasure and to submit to moral weakness.

In psychodynamic terms, the officer consciously experiences conflict between succumbing to the immoral pleasure of feeling that he is immune from the rules and his conscience which constantly reminds him that he is indeed bound by rules of conduct. At his unconscious level of experience, the policeman's ego is torn between satisfying the demands of his id for all the pleasure that his special status and power can get for it and his superego which constantly requires him to renounce any pleasure that is not obtained from following the rules. The resulting unconscious emotion is one of guilt. The officer feels guilt for wanting to disobey his superego by disregarding its prohibitions.

The policeman worries that the gratification he receives from the power he has is morally wrong. He should not feel so good about terrible things. He should not get a pleasurable rush from the street, he should only feel a sense of moral satisfaction from trying to uphold the law. In short he must be the altruistic cop described by Kirkham (1974). He should only derive the feeling of being satisfied with himself for doing the right thing; but the policeman knows that he gets a great deal of emotional gratification from the street. Consequently, the policeman must grapple with the unconscious experience of guilt because he wants the pleasure of feeling powerful and being above the rules. It is not an exaggeration to suggest that every policeman has used his power for its own sake rather than to uphold the law on at least one occasion. The ensuing feeling of guilt for having disregarded his moral code is nearly universal among police officers. I believe that this shared guilt for being seduced by the pleasure of using power for its own sake is one of the contributing factors in the police fraternity's reliance on secrecy.

At the risk of waxing literary, the fundamental conflict the policeman faces is much like the one endured by Kurtz, the missionary in Conrad's (1950) *Heart of Darkness*. Kurtz went into the jungle as a missionary only to discover that power over others was a stronger source of pleasure than civilizing the natives. Kurtz discovered that the virtues of self-denial and self-sacrifice were no match for the visceral pleasures of exercising power. Similar discoveries were described by Vietnam war combat soldiers who experienced the emotional rush of being in battle (Herr, 1977; Broyles, 1986).

A question frequently asked by recruits and young policemen is, "How can I keep the street from rubbing off on me?" They are aware of the dehumanizing potential of coping with the misery and disillusionment of the work and are apprehensive of being dehumanized themselves. To rely on one of Baker's cops once again:

> from the time a guy puts on the uniform and steps out of the academy, an erosion process begins to take place. Some guys are able to cope with it fine.... That's very, very rare. The vast majority of policemen are eroded by the environment, by the people and places they work in. They become reflections of the people they police. (Baker, 1986, p. 300)

This observation is only partly correct. It states the policeman's fear that the street will erode his moral and spiritual values through constant exposure to degradation and misery and his feeling helpless to change it. As I have said this is a real, legitimate fear of being overwhelmed by evil. However, the part that is missing is that he also worries that rather than his becoming a reflection of the people he polices, the people are a reflection of *him*.

He worries that his pleasure from being in the street means that he is no different from the criminal element that derives pleasure and meaning from the street as well. There seems to be a more difficult question that the policeman asks of no one but himself: "How can I keep 'the street' that is inside me from coming out and taking me over?"

Steve Ryder, a journalist and former cop, describes how he became so totally immersed in the job that he could not leave the street out of the rest of his life. The cop, according to Ryder, fights a "war against his own sensitivities, [against] his sense of humanity" (p. 62). On the surface, this appears to be a description of the familiar explanation of the job rubbing off on the man. But Ryder goes on to explain that it is the gratification of the job, namely, danger and power, that undermined his emotional ability to continue to live in the civilian world after his tour:

> the boy-man who joined the force has become the man-boy playing real cops with real robbers and real guns, and is playing the game well—to win. He isn't a bad guy. He is, in fact, a damn good cop. But he lives in a world that ordinary people seldom visit. Once you've been there, you can't go home again. (1979, p. 62)

Ryder's reference to "boy-man" and "man-boy" speaks directly to the capacity of the job to gratify childhood fantasies of omnipotence and to become addictive. Power and danger become the most important vehicles to pleasure if the policeman cannot successfully resist this addiction.

If we look at Ryder's courageous self-examination as a narrative of how he gave into the pleasure of the work, then we can see that the policeman's worry is not only that hating the street will destroy his sense of humanity. It is also the fear that loving the street too much will bring out the worst in him until he is no different from the antisocial criminals with whom he contends.

The addictive rush created by the emotional experience of power and its effect on a cop's behavior can be inferred from studies that have categorized police behavior into specific types. One type of behavior is labeled the "Enforcer" by Muir (1977). The Enforcer, according to Muir, is most likely to rely on threats and coercion as a general strategy to handle any type of problem in the street. He is comfortable using coercion because he has rejected "the ethical concerns of civilization. There would be no guilt because there would be *no conscience*" [my emphasis] (p. 50). The enforcer has no moral conflict about using force because he has given up his morality against using unnecessary coercion. In short, he has given in to the pleasure of using power. Muir describes the Enforcer as turning routine situations into dangerous ones so that he winds up using force to quell them. Why would a cop actively make a nonviolent encounter into a hostile one? My answer by now should be obvious: he wants to feel the pleasure of using his power.

Brown (1981) devised another typology of police behavior on patrol. He calls one type the "Clean Beat Crime Fighter":

> He is something of a rogue elephant in a police department, the kind of officer who will make a lot of felony arrests but will be consistently in trouble. The Clean Beat patrolman thus lives in a continual state of tension: his proclivity for aggressive action conflicts with the demands imposed by an increasingly watchful department and a hostile public. He is, in a word, frustrated. (p. 230)

The Clean Beat cop is frustrated because he needs action—he needs the rush and feels distress without it. He is hooked on the street. Unless he gets the rush of pleasure he feels increasingly agitated. Like the Enforcer in Muir's typology, the Clean Beat Crime Fighter handles minor disputes with threats of force and resorts to arrest rather than mediation. As Brown says, the Clean Beat cop tends "to apply coercion spontaneously and very often indiscriminately" because he does not have the ability to regulate his aggressiveness (1981, p. 232). As a result he is in a frenzy looking for action because he cannot contain his need for the emotional gratification that only the use of power can provide.

Brown's description of the Clean Beat cop's frenzy is supported by a policeman's recounting of his own frenzied search for action:

> When you're looking for [action], you never find it. You come back and your eyes are like two cigaret burns in a blanket, sick of looking for people to do something. You wish mayhem on some poor little old lady walking down the street. I wish this guy would grab her purse and knock her down so I could grab him. (Baker, 1986, p. 305)

Brown suggests that the Clean Beat cop's behavior results from his literal acceptance of the values of police professionalism. His absolutist view of law enforcement causes him, says Brown, to have a simplistic view of his job as enforcing every law to the maximum.

The Clean Beat cop bears considerable resemblance to Reiser's (1974) description of the "John Wayne Syndrome" in new police officers. The symptoms of this syndrome are "cynicism, over-seriousness, emotional withdrawal and coldness, authoritarian attitudes, and the development of tunnel vision in which values become dichotomized into all or nothing" (1974, p. 158). Reiser believes this behavior is caused by peer group pressure to be a tough cop and by the need to ward off external threats and internal emotional reactions that would leave him highly anxious. Another symptom belonging to the John Wayne Syndrome is emotional distancing and coolness toward the officer's wife and family and an intense identification and emotional involvement with peers.

The psychodynamic explanation for the behavior of Muir's "Enforcer," Brown's "Clean Beat Cop," and Reiser's "John Wayne Syndrome" is that the emotional gratification this type of policeman receives from the job is so intense and desirable that he cannot detach himself from the behavior that provides him with this pleasure. In each type, the officer's behavior is oriented around the exercise of power and the use of aggression. It is behavior that brings about the rush of excitement and pleasure that the policeman cannot do without.

Reiser (1974) also suggests that the syndrome is partly a defense against becoming aware of painful emotions experienced in the street. In other words, it is the emotional withdrawal and seeming indifference to feeling helpless that is labeled "police cynicism." I believe that the policeman manifesting the John Wayne Syndrome is not emotionally withdrawn at all. He is caught up with feeling powerful. Any civilian who has endured dealing with a John Wayne policeman will not describe him as emotionally withdrawn but as contemptuous and condescending. He is anything but detached and indifferent: he is letting the civilian know that he is "the boss: and the civilian is "the shithead" (Baker, 1986, p. 343).

Neither the Enforcer, the Clean Beat Cop, nor John Wayne would ever consciously admit that they are in love with power, but they are. In fact, they love the job so much they cannot leave it at the end of the tour. The emotional detachment from loved ones is more complex than just choosing to identify with other cops. It is the result of the policeman's dissatisfaction with being a husband who must be affectionate and caring instead of a cop who is powerful and tough. The idea of being loving, soft, and vulnerable is now unrewarding to a man who knows the pleasure of the street.

Wambaugh gives us a clear perspective of the disparity between the gratification of the street and the temptation to renounce intimacy and love because they do not match up to the street. In *The Blue Knight* (Wambaugh, 1979), Bumper Morgan's alter ego, Cruz Segovia, tries to convince Morgan that he needs to love because "the street causes the police officer to lose belief in the important values. I still believe them because I want to. I can come home, and the [street] isn't real" (1979, p. 135). Segovia felt that Morgan was in psychological danger because he relied on the job rather than on a love relationship for his emotional needs.

Wambaugh's point is that giving up the pleasure derived from power and aggressiveness for love and revealing one's weaknesses is a difficult choice for the police officer. The new cop who feels the adrenaline rush in the street may have a difficult time not behaving as if he were still on patrol in his own home. Unconsciously he may choose to treat his wife as if she were a "civilian" instead of the woman he loves because he does not want to become "ordinary" after work. He unconsciously becomes John Wayne—strong, tough, totally self-sufficient, and a loner—because that's who he is in the street and that's who he wants to remain. As usual, a policeman says it best: "The street is very seductive and very sensual. You may take it home with you because you want to take it home" (Baker, 1986, p. 19). There is the real temptation to bring the "prostitute," the police officer's pleasurable behavior in the street, home with him because he does not want to let it go and to have to accept the role of being an affectionate and vulnerable husband and a nurturing father. Being the husband and father look far less gratifying and far more depriving than does being a street cop.

This chapter has sought to focus on the police officer's extraordinarily complex emotional involvement with his work. He consciously feels hatred for the work because it overwhelms him with feelings of misery and powerlessness. At the same time, he consciously feels love for the work because of its capacity to make him feel heroic and special. These emotions have a major effect on the policeman's conscious experience of himself and others. The work also has a profound impact on his unconscious emotions. It makes him feel shame for having failed to live up to his ego ideal, yet it provides him with considerable pleasure because the job enables him to satisfy the demands of his ego ideal.

Compounding the emotional complexity of the policeman's feelings for his work is the conflict between the fundamental pleasure he receives from exercising power over others and his conscience. Consciously he feels torn between feeling good and being good. Unconsciously his conflict is between his wish to pursue the pleasure of being above the rules of behavior and the guilt he feels for wanting to disobey the moral dictates of his superego.

Since so much of his emotional involvement is unconscious, much of the police officer's conflicts are least accessible to logic and therefore not modified simply by consciously trying to neutralize them. As a result, they are resistant to conscious awareness and modification. Only insight into one's internal emotional life can bring about awareness and change.

Chapter 5

How Cops React to Ambivalence

Previous chapters have focused on the ambivalence of others toward the police officer and on the police officer's ambivalence toward others and the work itself. In this chapter we will focus on the police officer's psychological responses to ambivalence from others and from within himself.

REACTIONS TO THE AMBIVALENCE OF OTHERS

Chapter 2 examined the ambivalent feelings of the public, the police department, family, friends, and fellow officers toward the cop. Now we will look at his conscious and unconscious emotional responses and his behavioral reactions to their ambivalence.

The Public

The civilian's unconscious feeling that the policeman is an omnipotent, loving parent would appear to be an attitude the cop would welcome. Adulation and hero worship would certainly satisfy the officer's need for recognition and reinforce his superior status vis-à-vis the public. However, this worship of the cop as all-powerful, good parent has a catch, and the catch is that in the eyes of the civilian the cop cannot fail precisely because he can do everything. Unconsciously, the civilian in need loves the cop because the civilian sees him as infallible. Should the cop not make everything better, the civilian feels not only disappointment but also hate, because he or she believes the omnipotent cop has malevolently decided not to use his powers to make everything better. The civilian then unconsciously believes the cop is an all-powerful bad parent who inflicts suffering rather than removing it. In essence, the passing grade for the cop to be loved is 100 percent; anything less than total gratification brings on hate.

It does not take long for the policeman to realize that he is in a "no-win" situation because he is all too aware that he cannot be omnipotent. He knows that inevitably he will be regarded by the civilian as cruel and sadistic. In psychological language, this no-win dilemma is called a double bind (Bateson, 1960). The cop's unconscious emotional reaction to the double bind is identical to that of anyone in this trap—anxiety. One becomes anxious when he or she feels helpless in the face of a threat. Being in a situation in which the probability of failure is 100 percent makes the policeman anxious, so the civilian's hero worship and its concomitant demand for perfection causes the cop unconsciously to feel anxiety instead of pleasure.

The typical response to anxiety created by a double bind is emotional withdrawal. In facing an insoluble problem, a simple coping device is to remove one's self from being emotionally involved in trying to solve it. In sports jargon, one forfeits the game rather than loses it. Rather than trying to be Superman for the civilian and inevitably failing, the cop pulls back emotionally from the civilian's love so that he will not feel anxious about the certainty of losing that love and having it turned into hate. So, at an unconscious level anxiety is warded off by emotional withdrawal.

As a result of coping with anxiety by emotionally withdrawing, the officer's conscious experience is a sense of indifference. The policeman feels no emotional involvement with the civilian, feels no gratification for being treated as Superman, feels no anxiety about failing to be Superman, and feels no pain for being hated. In a word, the cop feels nothing for or about the civilian, and he regards the civilian as being of no emotional significance to him. His overt behavior is based on his conscious feelings of indifference. Consequently, when responding to a civilian's request for help, he does not feel anything when the civilian treats him with awe, nor does he react emotionally should worship change to rage because he cannot make the civilian happy and secure. He adopts the motto, "consider the source," when viewed with either reverence or hostility.

When incurring a rebellious civilian's hate for giving a summons or making an arrest, the policeman also feels anxiety, but it is caused by a very different threat than that of losing love. His anxiety is caused by feeling potentially overwhelmed by his own rage at the civilian. The cop is under orders to use the minimum force necessary to perform his job and faces departmental and possibly legal sanctions should he disobey them. He cannot give into his desire to wipe the floor with a civilian who freely expresses his rage without fear of reprisal. Unconsciously, the officer is anxious because he feels he may not be able to control his aggression and avoid subsequent departmental punishment.

This dilemma again is a double-bind situation, for the cop is in a no-win trap. If he restrains his aggression successfully, he feels humiliated by the civilian's insults and emasculated for not acting on his aggressive response to being insulted. If he gives in to his aggressive impulses, he faces severe punishment by the department. In this no-win dilemma, emotional withdrawal is also relied on as a quick and seemingly effective coping device. The cop unconsciously withdraws from being emotionally caught up with the civilian in order to maintain control over his rage and his power. Consequently his conscious experience is one of indifference to the insults. By having no emotional impact on him, the civilian is seen as insignificant, as not being important enough to warrant any emotional response. It is as though the police officer were a powerful adult dealing with a small child.

The police officer's behavior in this encounter reflects his conscious experience of feeling uninvolved. Having to interact with the civilian appears to be beneath him, just as an adult might feel about having to put up with someone else's crying child. It is not surprising in light of the officer's unconscious reliance on emotional withdrawal to alleviate anxiety that his overt behavior appears detached and indifferent to the adoring civilian in distress or to the angry civilian receiving a summons.

In both cases the policeman cannot risk emotional involvement because anxiety is an inevitable consequence. The public, however, does not interpret his detachment as a defense against anxiety. The public perceives his behavior as proof that cops are not human because they have no feelings, and that they do not care for anyone but other cops.

Some researchers (Reiser, 1974; Violanti, 1981) believe that the police department is largely responsible for police officers becoming "impersonal and hardened toward others" (Violanti, 1981, p. 94) through its treatment of police officers as things rather than people. The department also demands that its officers maintain an objective and dispassionate demeanor in order to keep control of events (Harris, 1973; Reiser, 1974) and to achieve standardized police behavior (Violanti, 1981).

My impression is that the department is getting a bad rap on this issue. The department's attempt to remove individuality from its members by seeking uniformity of behavior does not produce emotional withdrawal, but instead produces hostility and strong emotional ties with peers. Policemen do not become emotionally detached and then develop an indifferent style of relating to civilians because of the department's attempt to suppress their individuality. They react this way because it helps them remain unaware of feeling threatened by demands that they be superhuman or by assaults on their authority.

The Police Department

The department's ambivalent attitude toward the police officer is perplexing and difficult for him to contend with. As described in Chapter 2, the department tells the cop he is a well-trained professional who can handle any situation and who can use his discretion to cope with any difficult problem. On the other hand the department tells him he is not to question orders, that he cannot think for himself, that he is no different from all other officers, and that he needs close supervision to keep him from messing things up.

The officer's unconscious response to the department's positive attitude is to feel loved and appreciated as the preferred child (Symonds, 1973). However, these feelings are destined to be short-lived since he will lose the department's love and appreciation once he cannot meet its demands for perfection. The dilemma the cop faces with the department is emotionally very similar to the one presented by the public: perfection is expected, indeed, demanded as a condition for love, and if he cannot meet this demand, then the emotional response is hostility. However, unlike his relationship with the civilian in which he is regarded as a powerful parent, in his relationship with the department the policeman is viewed as the good or bad child, and the department is the omnipotent parent who demands perfection.

It is not unusual for policemen to talk of receiving citations from the department for outstanding service one week only to be reprimanded the next week for not following proper procedure. The department validates the cop's belief that he will be hated and punished once he shows any imperfection. In that case, the department regards him as too inept to follow proper procedure, too stupid to use good judgment, and too childlike to work independently. As with the public, the department's love is given only when the cop is all-knowing, all-powerful, and always right.

In short, the department regards him as a disobedient child and it treats him like one. The department is the powerful adult and the cop is now the bad child who requires punishment so that he will learn not to be bad. Formal letters of reprimand, reassignment to undesirable duty, suspension, or worse are the ways in which the department expresses its anger toward the officer for not living up to its expectations.

The policeman's unconscious reaction to being in this no-win situation is to feel anxious. He will receive the department's love only if he is perfect and its punishment when he inevitably makes a mistake. To ward off the anxiety created by his fear of losing the department's love, the officer relies on the defense mechanism of denial. By denying that the department has any concern for his well-being or has any positive regard for him, the cop can then deny that he has anything to lose. He does not have to worry about losing the department's love because the department has no love to offer—it only has hate for him. Denial permits the officer to escape feeling anxious by compelling him to view the department as his enemy. He is aware only of the department's punitive side and is blind to any action that would reflect any positive departmental attitude toward him. The officer's behavior resulting from his conscious one-dimensional experience of hostility from the department is to maintain a staunch distrust of everything the department says and does. He develops a cynical attitude toward the department's motives and actions because it is his adversary. The cop is likely to suspect any action taken by the department as inherently punitive.

Here is a veteran supervisor's description of the policeman's emotional perception of the department:

> The cops have no understanding of institutional realities or bureaucracy. They don't know how to talk to it, they don't know how it operates. Anything that it does, as far as they are concerned, is fucking them.
>
> They in no way could understand why the department would do what it does. They are disconnected—they are strangers to their own bureaucracy. Because they have no familiarity with bureaucracy, they give it too much credit. They think it has a diabolical design to fuck them.

As a result, policemen react toward any change in the department with the belief that it must be bad for them. For example, if a cop is assigned for specialized training, he will wonder if the department is sending him because it believes he is deficient in performing some aspect of his job. He concludes that specialized training really is remedial training for him because he needs to do better.

This attitude toward the department as a hypocritical and punitive opponent is often described as a form of police cynicism. The tendency to look for the worst in the police department and to deny anything good about it has been viewed as a result of being in the position of having no input into making decisions that affect how the police officer does his job. Of course this description is valid, but once again it needs to be complemented by a psychodynamic explanation to be more complete.

The psychodynamic explanation for the cop's cynical attitude toward the department is that it enables him to avoid the anxiety he must feel if he acknowledges the department's capacity to gratify him. If he says the department can do nothing good for him and is singularly hostile to him, then he can avoid the anxiety caused by the threat of losing the department's love and admiration. The result is that the officer has a unitary emotional response to the department—anger—and thus protects himself from feeling insecure about wanting the department to love him and being rejected for not being perfect enough to keep that love. It is no wonder then that cops will gather together and berate the police department for being arbitrary, inconsistent, uncaring, incompetent, and, most of all, malevolent toward its men.

A few policemen use reaction formation in just the opposite fashion. They unconsciously deny any shortcomings in the department's treatment of them in order to maintain an idealized view of the department as a perfect, benevolent parent. They consciously view the department as always being right and always knowing what is best for its cops. They do not question or disagree with policy because it must be obeyed without question. These men are committed to pleasing their supervisors by their exemplary behavior and eagerness to do the department's bidding. In short, they see the department as only the benevolent parent who is caring and eager to gratify them when they are good.

For these men who unconsciously select this response, the going can get very rough. There are two negative consequences to denying the department's hostility. The first is ostracism by brother officers. Being labeled a "brown nose" or "ass kisser" is second only to being called a coward by a cop's peers. Men who appear too cooperative, too compliant, too eager to please are shunned by other cops as being self-serving hypocrites who would sell out their dignity and masculinity to get ahead. Often an eager-to-please rookie is told in rather blunt terms that kissing ass is frowned upon by the fraternity, and that if he wants to have any friends on his job (and possibly any back up), he had better change his ways.

The second negative outcome to using positive reaction formation is the inevitability that the department will punish even the obedient, compliant cop for not behaving perfectly. When the cop who gives 150 percent is still reprimanded, he feels all his good behavior has counted for nothing because only his errors are noticed. At this point the positive reaction formation defense becomes untenable and is often replaced by an intense negative reaction formation as a defense. Given the hazards involved, it is not surprising that reaction formation which denies the department's hostility is employed by a small percentage of police in dealing with the department's ambivalent attitude and treatment of its officers.

Family

Being on the receiving end of mixed emotions from loved ones is difficult for everyone, but for the policeman there are additional issues that make it even more difficult to cope. When he gets love and affection from his wife, he feels both gratified and relieved since here is someone who loves him for himself, not because he is perfect. She is proud of her "knight in shining armor," just as he is—he need be no more than himself to make her proud of him and happy being with him.

The cop accepts her pride and love with great enthusiasm because he feels he does not have to do anything more to keep her loving him. He believes her love is unconditional with no strings attached. Unlike the public, his wife does not require him to earn her love. Therefore, the policeman comes to believe that he cannot lose her love and affection precisely because he regards it as being given unconditionally.

The problem for him is that love rarely exists without anger. Almost everyone has mixed feelings about loved ones. So, when his wife gets angry at him for being a cop because his job deprives her of having him home at night and on holidays, or it makes her feel left out of a large and important part of his life, or it confines her social life to being with the families of other policemen, he is taken by surprise and feels betrayed. She has withdrawn her love and has become hostile to him because he is a cop after having loved him for being a cop.

The policeman feels hurt, and the only way to reduce the probability of being hurt again is to withdraw. He withdraws emotionally from his wife without being aware of it, so that consciously he sees no difference in the way he reacts to her. If she accuses him of being distant and cold, he will feel that she is once again treating him unfairly and withdraw even more. A vicious cycle is set in motion in which his withdrawal leads to her anger which then causes him to withdraw further.

The same pattern develops with respect to the officer's children. Their unconditional love and admiration for him is accepted by him as enduring. As his kids reach adolescence, they feel ostracized or held to a higher standard of obedience because their father is a cop. They become angry at him for putting them in this stigmatized position. In defense, the officer unconsciously withdraws his emotional involvement with them. After his withdrawal provokes angry comments from them that he is both physically and emotionally unavailable, he withdraws even further.

Unlike his reaction to the civilian's ambivalence, the cop's emotional withdrawal does not cause him to treat his family with indifference. He cannot deny that they are important to him and that he values their love a great deal. His withdrawal leads to conscious feelings of being unappreciated and mis-understood because he has chosen to be a police officer. He comes to believe that his family's love comes with an enor-mous string attached, and that string is a demand that he not be who he is—a cop.

Friends

When a man becomes a policeman, his friends uncon-sciously view him as more powerful and more capable than they are. He is no longer a peer but a caring, benevolent par-ental figure. It is not uncommon for friends to ask a police officer to intercede on their behalf in disputes with neighbors or with a local government agency. He is now their powerful ally who is always available to help. This emotional percep-tion of the policeman causes the same anxiety in him as the public's hero worship does, because sooner or later he will fail them or tell them he cannot help them. Their response will be to accuse him of being callous and indifferent.

It also happens that when a man becomes a policeman, his friends resent his greater power and authority and their own anxiety at feeling inferior to him. Negative attitudes from friends who no longer view the policeman as the nice guy they used to know causes him not only to withdraw from them for self-protection but also to reject them in retaliation for their hostility. In rejecting his former friends, the officer consigns them to the category of "civilian," a group he regards as ignorant, hostile, and ungrateful.

The result of withdrawing from and denigrating former friends is the officer's progressive self-imposed isolation from civilians and a stronger bonding with other police officers. Rather than feel put upon by friends who treat him with am-bivalence, he seeks the friendship of peers from whom he does not consciously feel any sense of ostracism. In this way he also protects himself from the pain of feeling rejected by consciously rejecting them. In essence he says, "I quit," instead of hearing them say, "You're out of the group."

Other Police Officers

The fact that his estrangement from the civilian world drives the cop further into the police subculture does not mean that his peers treat him with unconditional love. As described in Chapter 2, the officer's peers treat him with ambivalence that takes the form of hostility to any qualities he may have which they feel are soft, weak, and cowardly.

The cop's unconscious response to the peer group's expression of ambivalence is to feel anxiety. He wards off being aware of his anxiety by denying that the peer group is hostile and potentially punitive. The mechanism of denial permits him to have the conscious experience of being only loved and cared for by brother officers, and the belief that their love is constant and will never be taken from him. He is not consciously aware that their love is conditional and will be removed and replaced by rejection should he not behave according to their expectations. The officer's denial of his peers' hostility is the mirror opposite of his denial of the department's love.

The need to deny other cops' hostility and to be aware only of their acceptance and support requires the officer to deny any personal qualities he has that may be unacceptable to his brother officers. The unconscious denial of softness, reflection and empathy is required in order to successfully maintain his denial that his fellow policemen will hate him for having these qualities. This intrapsychic "domino theory" says he must deny he has these "bad" qualities so that he can deny his brother officers' hostility. If he is only "good," then he gets only love.

The policeman's resultant behavior is predicated on his unconscious denial of being "bad," that is, compassionate and thoughtful. He begins to throw off these qualities so that he behaves as his peers expect: he becomes tough and unfeeling. Many police officers describe this emotional metamorphosis as something that simply overtook them by surprise. It was not until loved ones repeatedly pointed out that they were no longer behaving in the kind, compassionate ways they used to before coming on the job that these men realized they had indeed changed from being soft civilians to tough cops.

The officers then conclude that the street has changed them. Of course this is true; the street has a profound emotional impact on their behavior. However, it is not just the street that requires them to regard empathy and self-reflection as undesirable personal attributes. The demands of the peer group also require the policeman to renounce the soft aspects of his self-identity to remain a member in good standing in the police fraternity.

THE POLICE OFFICER'S OWN AMBIVALENCE

The policeman's mixed feelings of love and hate toward the public, the department, family and friends, and peers were described in Chapter 3. In this section we will explore his emotional reactions to his own ambivalence and the behavior that they bring about.

The Public

The police officer unconsciously sees the public as the source of gratification of his need to be admired as a hero. At the same time he also feels the citizenry is nothing more than a mass of weak, dependent, ungrateful inferiors. These polar opposite attitudes toward the public, namely, the source of recognition and admiration versus hostility and condescension, exist side by side in the unconscious mind of the police officer.

The policeman attempts to cope with his simultaneous feelings of love and hate by isolating them into separate feelings having nothing to do with each other. He compartmentalizes his mixed feelings in order to not feel any internal conflict and resultant anxiety caused by his mixed feelings. As a result of the unconscious use of isolation, the policeman can hold both positive and negative feelings about the public without feeling conflict.

Before the television camera, he may truly want the public to appreciate and admire him. On patrol he may truly feel all the people around him are his inferiors. Both attitudes are real for the police officer, but he has trouble consciously recognizing that both feelings exist.

The Police Department

The policeman's love for the police department as omnipotent benevolent parent is problematic because it casts him in the role of a child seeking love from a remote parent who demands perfect behavior before showing him love. In a word, his love is dangerous because it sets him up for feeling constantly rejected for never being perfect.

Since the probability of winning the department's love is low and keeping it is nil, the policeman again is faced with a no-win situation. To avoid feeling anxious from being trapped in this no-win situation, the typical cop isolates his feelings of love and hate.

Isolation allows him to compartmentalize his ambivalence so that he can work hard to be promoted to sergeant, to make detective, or to get a prestigious assignment with the expectation that the department will recognize his good work and reward him. He will then experience the department's reward as love. These positive feelings have no connection to the hate he also feels for the department for being punitive, hypocritical, self-serving, and cowardly.

As a result of using isolation, most cops work hard for promotion or commendations while at the same time they rage against the higher-ups for being stupid, insensitive cowards. They have unconsciously compartmentalized their opposite feelings so that each has no influence on the other. Their conscious feelings are therefore also divided into separate experiences that do not affect each other. It is as if there are two police departments—one good and one bad—rather than one department for whom they have mixed feelings.

Some policemen unconsciously rely on reaction formation rather than isolation to keep from feeling anxious. In using reaction formation, these officers unconsciously deny their feeling of both love and hate and are conscious of only one or the other. Most cops relying on reaction formation unconsciously deny their love for the department. They hate the police department with a vengeance. The behavior that results from this hate ranges from verbal barrages of outrage at supervisors and administrators to acts of sabotage through passive-aggressive maneuvers (Symonds, 1973).

Passive-aggressive behavior is characterized by the "resistance to demands for adequate performance in occupational or social functioning; the resistance is expressed indirectly rather than directly...such individuals are passively expressing covert aggression" (American Psychiatric Association, 1980, p. 328). How does a cop passively express his aggression so that he cannot be accused of deliberately breaking the rules? Well, the average policeman has a number of ways to tweak the department's nose and get away with it.

He can take every single sick day the contract permits, or he can make a bullshit arrest in the last hour of his tour and collect a lot of overtime to process the arrest, which will probably be dismissed. He can constantly call for a supervisor to handle a problem rather than tackling it himself, or he can spend a great deal of time "handling" a routine call, thereby making himself unavailable for more calls. In fact, for a creative angry policeman the list of passive-aggressive maneuvers is virtually endless because he can use his vast discretionary powers to do nothing or even to mess things up as long as he technically follows procedure.

Some researchers (Ellison & Genz, 1978; Maslach & Jackson, 1979) believe these passive-aggressive reactions are indicators of burnout caused by the police officer's repeated exposure to tragedy and misery that he cannot prevent or repair. To be sure, burn out does happen among police officers, but relying on it to explain passive-aggressive behavior is incorrect. Emotionally burned-out people do not want to fight; they want to be left alone, to withdraw. The cop who tries to sabotage the department with its own regulations is retaliating in response to feeling abused; he is not withdrawing to lick his wounds. He has by no means surrendered emotionally; he is carrying out a vigorous guerrilla war against a powerful enemy.

Family

The policeman's ambivalent feelings toward his wife are most complex. The love he feels for her is in large part based on seeing her as an adoring, delicate lady who needs his strength and protection. But his love turns to anger if she depends on him to the point where he feels she is weak, incompetent, and demanding, as if she were a civilian in distress.

Conversely, he loves her when she takes care of things on her own so that he does not feel burdened by family problems after having to handle problems at work. But he feels angry if she becomes so self-reliant that she no longer sees him as her knight in shining armor but as her equal. At this point she is no longer giving him the hero worship that made him feel love for her.

The principal coping device for dealing with his mixed feelings is the now-familiar defense mechanism of reaction formation. Since there is no conflict in acknowledging love for his wife, the officer unconsciously denies the hate he feels, thus warding off the conflict and resulting anxiety. One indication of reaction formation is the tendency of many policemen to overdo the role of knight and family protector by curtailing their wife's activities to reduce her susceptibility to crime

(Stratton, 1984). It is not uncommon for a police wife to complain that she feels confined by her husband's preoccupation with her safety and control of where and when she may go.

The cop's unconscious denial of his anger also causes him to feel hurt even more by his wife's hostility. Her anger at him seems even more undeserved because he believes that all the hostility is hers, not his. As a result, his withdrawal from her seems not only justified to him, it also appears that she forced him to withdraw from her unwarranted attack.

The officer also relies on reaction formation to deal with his ambivalence toward his children. He denies that he is angry with them for not providing the hero worship they once did and is aware only of his love for them. As he does with his wife, the policeman tries to keep a close rein on his children's activities. Often he is so restrictive that the children rebel by doing exactly what he told them not to do. They flaunt it as a gesture of independence. Their willful disobedience, like his wife's anger, causes him to feel unloved and unappreciated, and he then emotionally insulates himself from them.

Friends

In grappling with his mixed feeling toward civilian friends, the policeman uses projection as a defense against anxiety. In essence, he unconsciously projects his hostility and contempt onto them, thus allowing himself to acknowledge consciously that they are rejecting him, not that he is rejecting them. This defense mechanism is reinforced by the reality that they have hostile feelings toward him because of his power and authority. The officer thus sees himself as having been sent into exile by his civilian friends. What he does not acknowledge is that his exile is in part self-imposed. His rejection of them for being less capable, less powerful, and less self-reliant is denied.

As a result, policemen recite a kind of litany about the friends they had before they went on the job. They say that their former friends turned their backs on them once they entered the academy. This is true, but it is not the whole story. The police officer also turns his back on old friends but denies it and places all the rejecting feelings on them. It is a rare policeman who openly says he does not like socializing with civilian friends because they seem too naive about the real world of the street, that they seem to know so little of what people are capable of doing to others and to themselves, and that they seem too soft and too comfortable to deal with danger. As one of Wambaugh's insightful cops noted,

> pretty soon you won't be able to feel the same way about your friends in the lodge or church or in your neighborhood because they won't measure up to policemen in these ways. You'll be able to come up with a quick solution for any kind of strange situation because you have to do it everyday, and you'll get mad as hell at your old friends if they can't. (1970, p. 81)

Most policemen consciously think they wanted to remain with the old crowd but were ostracized for coming on the job. Their conscious experience is more palatable than their denied attitude of superiority toward their old friends. Attributing the end of former friendships to being rejected once he became a cop makes a police officer feel that he has not changed, but that his friends have. In fact, he *has* changed a great deal since he became a cop. He now feels that he is more powerful and capable than his old civilian friends.

Other Police Officers

The principal defense mechanism used by the policeman to cope with ambivalent feelings toward brother officers is identification. The mechanism of identification involves denying hostile feelings toward a loved person and absorbing characteristics of that person. For example, children unconsciously internalize the qualities of their parents and make those qualities their own. Kids imitate the mannerisms of their parents by unconsciously identifying with them and behaving like them. Many parents are surprised to hear themselves speak to their children with the same words their father or mother spoke to them. However, this experience is only part of the surprise. The other part is that many of these parents had previously made a conscious promise not to speak to their kids as their parents had spoken to them. So, even though they had consciously promised themselves not to behave like their parents, unconsciously they had internalized their parents' mannerisms and made them their own. The unconscious mechanism by which this internalization and imitation takes place is identification.

Identification is a powerful mechanism in the policeman's coping response to his own mixed feelings toward other cops. He represses the feeling of hostility toward brother officers and internalizes the qualities he sees in his peers. He becomes like the cops in the peer group whom he admires and does not want to antagonize by being angry with them. The officer unconsciously imitates the cops he admires and becomes like them.

The whole issue of identification with fellow officers is an important one because it may help clarify some of the more perplexing problems in police work such as the powerful influence of academy instructors and field-training officers on the self-concept of recruits and rookies. Identification also plays a part in rapid transition from civilian to loyal member of the police family. In the early stages of training, many recruits say with conviction that they will not let the job change· their personality or values. But by the end of a few weeks of field training, they come back to the academy acting and sounding very much like the cops to whom they were assigned. When informed that they have changed, these recruits seem genuinely surprised that the very thing they vowed would never happen did indeed take place without their being aware of it.

The identification mechanism also explains in part why police officers prefer to spend their leisure time with other cops rather than with civilians. By defining themselves as members of the peer group and assuming the characteristics of the group's definition of who and what a cop is, they no longer see any common qualities among themselves and their civilian friends.

It is important to bear in mind that identification is very different from conscious imitation. The purpose of identification is to prevent the intrusion of anxiety into the person's conscious experience by denying hate for a loved person and taking on the person's qualities. It is very different from deliberately deciding to act one way or another in order to receive affection from an individual or to belong to a group.

THE POLICE OFFICER'S AMBIVALENCE TOWARD THE WORK

Hatred for the Work

In Chapter 4, the policeman's exposure to human misery and degradation on a regular basis assaults his value system to the point that he finds it incredibly difficult to regard humanity as having or deserving any respect. To add insult to injury, the cop also feels overwhelmed by the worst aspects of human nature and powerless to overcome them. The feeling of powerlessness leads him to experience "objective anxiety." Objective anxiety is caused by a threat from the environment to the ego. In this case, the officer's capacity to cope with the misery of the street is endangered, and his unconscious response is objective anxiety.

In these circumstances the officer's anxiety stems from feeling overwhelmed by his own empathic emotional responses to seeing other human beings treated horribly, by the helpless rage he feels against those who have degraded their victims and escaped, and by the assault on his values of human dignity and goodness. His anxiety is partially caused by his own humanity, his ability to put himself in the victim's shoes (Martin *et al.*, 1986). The other cause of his anxiety is his feeling helpless to prevent people from committing such cruel crimes or to catch and punish them afterward.

Empathic pain is an occupational hazard in many helping professions, but it is particularly threatening in police work because it destroys the primary sources of gratification the officer seeks from the work: excitement, power, and heroism. He does not feel any pleasurable emotion when comforting victims or standing guard at homicides or suicides. He does not feel any sense of power knowing that the perpetrator is long gone or that the law is ineffective in dealing out appropriate punishment for particularly cruel acts of violence against helpless victims. And he knows that he will receive no hero worship from victims or the public, nor will the department reward him for coping with these emotionally wrenching situations. What he does feel is empathic pain for victims and an intense feeling of helplessness and rage for being unable to do anything to make things better.

Helplessness is one of the most frightening and painful feelings anyone can have, but for the policeman it is even more distressing since he sees himself as being powerful and therefore immune from feeling helpless. He cannot permit himself to feel helpless if he is to continue believing that he can handle anything in the street that comes his way.

Consequently the officer must avoid the anxiety caused by empathic emotional reactions and feelings of helplessness by removing these feelings from his conscious mind. In order to ward off awareness of empathic responses, the policeman uses denial as a defense. He unconsciously denies feeling pain for others by saying he does not feel anything or by ignoring the existence of another person's pain. Kroes (1976) calls this denial mechanism "numbing." The policeman consciously assumes an emotionally detached position in dealing with victims to prevent himself from having strong feelings for them. Gudjonsson and Adlam (1983) found that police officers in Great Britain have lower scores on empathy than do recruits. They concluded that police work causes a decline in empathy, regardless of how much time on the job the police officer has.

Intense emotions make the police officer anxious that he will be overcome by painful feelings. The mechanism of denial thus creates a behavioral response of detachment and a lack of concern for the victim. Much of the hostility directed at police by crime or accident victims is based on their perception of officers' indifference to their suffering and business-like attitude toward them when they are frightened and in pain.

The principal mechanism for defending against feeling helpless is projection. In using projection, the policeman is saying he is not powerless, but *those* people around him are powerless. The civilians are powerless, not he. He dumps what he feels inside onto those outside and says the feelings belong to them. Dumping his own negative feelings about himself onto civilians permits him to disown them. So, when someone is robbed or assaulted by yet another criminal who has gotten away, the policeman does not feel powerless. It is the victims, not he, who cannot defend themselves or cope with threats to their well-being.

Projection has enabled the policeman to remain oblivious to his feelings of helplessness and to be aware only of feeling powerful and superior to civilians. This feeling of superiority results in a cynical view of the civilian world and a sense of self-imposed detachment from it. His behavior may range from speaking to civilians with a contemptuous tone of voice to having no qualms about clocking an asshole who has not shown him sufficient respect. The underlying cause of the officer's cynical attitude, says Niederhoffer (1967), is his anxiety over feeling that he has failed:

> Anxious over a personal failure, the individual policeman often disguises his feelings with a cynical attitude, and thus negates the value of the prize he did not attain. Frequently he includes in his cynicism all persons who still seek that prize or have succeeded in winning it, and, occasionally, depreciates the entire social system in which the failure occurred. (p. 95)

It is very tempting for someone with power to use it with minimal provocation when he believes that his relatively powerless counterpart is too weak and worthless to be regarded as human. If people are not worth being treated with respect or compassion, it is all too easy for the officer to throw his weight around to reinforce his feeling of being more powerful than and superior to the public.

The pervasive problem of police officers using excessive force shows how easy it is for projection to influence aggressive behavior. Since the officer projects feelings of powerlessness and failure onto civilians, he then, says Niederhoffer, "feels justified and righteous in using power and toughness to perform his duties, [and] he feels like a martyr when he is charged with brutality and abuse of power" (1967, p. 118).

Finally, the police officer's basic beliefs in the essential dignity of man and the value of a code of moral behavior is assaulted, mugged if you will, by what he encounters in the street. Like the Vietnam vet described by Lifton in Chapter 4, the cop's whole notion of human nature and what constitutes good and bad is undermined in the street. His beliefs that people are essentially good and that he should follow the Golden Rule when dealing with people are emotionally blown away by the degradation to which people subject each other or themselves (Pope *et al.*, 1986).

He finds it threatening to his emotional stability to continue believing in human dignity under these conditions because this belief is pounded simply by his patrolling the streets. If his belief is assaulted, then he feels overwhelmed emotionally. The same danger applies to believing in the Golden Rule. He soon finds out that many people interpret courtesy as weakness and kindness as fear. Being courteous and kind to civilians too frequently invites insults and threats from them.

To cope with this shock to his basic values and the anxiety it creates, the policeman relies on the mechanism of reaction formation (Hilbert, 1978). Instead of consciously saying that his beliefs that human beings are essentially good and that treating them with kindness will be rewarded with kindness, he says, "I believe human beings are worthless and that they do not deserve kindness or respect." Wambaugh describes this defense from the cop's perspective:

it's not the capacity for evil that astounds young policemen. Rather it's the mind boggling worthlessness of
human beings. There's not enough dignity in mankind
for evil and that's the most terrifying thing a policeman
learns. (1976, p. 168)

In essence, the policeman disavows any belief in the worth of
human beings, instead of acknowledging that he does believe
in human dignity and living with the anxiety of having that
belief attacked. He also disavows the Golden Rule of conduct
for the same reason.

The use of reaction formation results in the conscious belief that he and his brother officers are not allies of the public
but rather enemies of the public. He has dignity and thus
deserves respect, but *they*, the civilians, do not (Lester, 1980).
As police psychologist Michael Roberts says, "Everything and
everybody else is at a distance. After three to five years on
the job, cops divide the world into two groups: assholes and
cops" (Meredith, 1984, p. 22). Jacobi (1975) is even more em-
phatic on this issue:

With increasing time spent in police work, the initial
moral idealism of the police cadet turns into a hard bit-
ten, bitter, and cynical orientation toward the world
where all one sees or expects is evil, filth and depravity,
particularly when this is coupled with the policeman's
growing social isolation from civilian society. This leads
him finally to feel that everyone outside is an "asshole"
and often leads to similar distrusting relations with his
fellow workers. (1975, p. 93)

Robert's view is consistent with Niederhoffer's (1967) position that police officers become progressively more cynical
with experience and are most cynical between seven and ten
years on the job. Researchers have had a difficult time defining
just what constitutes police cynicism (Rafky, 1975; Chandler
& Jones, 1979; Regoli & Poole, 1979; Regoli *et al.*, 1979; Holtzman, 1980; Anson *et al.*, 1986; Langworthy, 1987) because there
does not appear to be a consistent relationship between cynical attitudes and a policeman's behavior.

Niederhoffer (1967) says that cynicism is a product of socialization into a police subculture that espouses cynicism. However, cynicism does not necessarily affect the cop's performance of his duty. In fact, a study by Wilt and Bannon (1976) found that those police officers scoring higher on a cynicism scale had more commendations than did those with lower scores. O'Connell, Holzman, and Armandi (1986) suggest that police cynicism may not be a unidimensional but a multidimensional concept involving organizational cynicism and work cynicism. My view, like that of O'Connell and coworkers, is that cynicism is indeed a multidimensional concept, except that from a psychodynamic standpoint its components are "malignant" and "benign" cynicism.

Perhaps looking at cynicism as the byproduct of denial, projection, and reaction formation may clarify some of the confusion. The use of denial of empathic pain, of projection of feelings of helplessness, and of reaction formation against believing in human dignity are all involved in forming the constellation of attitudes that many call "police cynicism."

It is possible that the use of these defense mechanisms results in conscious cynical attitudes that permit the officer to do his job without enduring the anxiety that goes with it. Cynicism permits the officer to protect his emotional stability so that he can cope with the misery, degradation, and nihilism he encounters in the street. One can view cynicism as a complex of defense mechanisms, such as denial, isolation, projection, and reaction formation, whose purpose is to protect the cop from being overwhelmed by anxiety and pain.

The cynicism syndrome of numbing, feeling contempt for powerless victims and people in need, and believing that people are worthless appears to be very effective in allowing the policeman to go through horrible situations without "losing it." Cynicism thus may be a part of the police subculture's ethos because it is so easy to use and so effective in removing anxiety. However, relying on cynicism forces the cop to cut himself off from those emotions that make him feel connected to the people he polices and from his own humanity. In this sense, his cynicism has become malignant—it has become pervasive and has begun to kill off the healthier emotional parts of the officer's personality.

Since cynicism is so easy to use and effective in protecting him from feeling anxiety and pain on the job, the policeman may rely on it off the job to ward off feeling anxious or sad. He may begin to view the whole world as a sewer, not just his beat; he may be unable to feel compassion or affection for his wife and kids, particularly when they seem vulnerable or needy; he may rely on throwing his weight around at home to "solve" arguments; and he may withdraw from the whole civilian world because it is totally populated by assholes.

When the officer gets to this point, it is clear that his reliance on cynicism is now more harmful than the anxiety it prevents. The cop is now paying an enormous price for feeling strong and worthwhile through his use of cynicism: he has no feelings for anyone else. At this point he is an emotional "loner" (Niederhoffer, 1967). We might say that his malignant cynicism has spread to the point where he no longer can feel anything other than cynicism. Officers who feel emotionally numb may rely on alcohol to give them at least a brief period in which they have the capacity to feel. Perhaps the ritual of drinking after a tour allows these men to regain their emotional life.

If being cynical on the job works for the police officer, then he feels no emotional connection to the public. If he relies on cynicism both on and off the job, then the cop feels no emotional connection to anyone. If cynicism does not work for him on the job, he feels overwhelmed by anxiety, pain, helplessness, and nihilism; he becomes depressed and withdrawn in all areas of his life (American Psychiatric Association, 1980). The job becomes a source of unrelenting anxiety and emotional pain for which he has no remedy. He cannot function adequately on the job or break out of his misery off the job. The policeman for whom cynicism has not been effective can only try to avoid feeling distress by avoiding the job itself. He takes every available sick day, is rarely first on the scene of a disturbance, tries to push off calls onto the other cops, and looks the other way rather than issue a summons or make an arrest.

At this stage the police officer is in serious psychological trouble. Not only does he no longer feel capable of coping with the emotional damage brought about by the work, he does not feel able to cope with life. Many policemen in this dilemma try to alleviate their depression with alcohol as an emotional anesthetic from their depression. Unlike the overly cynical policeman who needs alcohol to have feelings, the depressed officer uses alcohol to numb his feelings of low self-esteem, powerlessness, and nihilism. More will be said about alcoholism as an occupational hazard in Chapter 7.

Love for the Work

As much as the police officer hates his job for the emotional and spiritual toll it takes on him, he also gets pleasure from feeling he has great power and immunity from the rules. However, this pleasure is experienced as "bad" rather than the "good" pleasure one feels from being virtuous. He must somehow ward off feeling anxious for having such a pleasurable time using his power in the midst of misery and suffering. This type of anxiety is called "superego anxiety" because the feelings of pleasure are seen as dangerous since they are immoral.

Superego anxiety differs from the anxiety brought about by feelings of empathic pain, powerlessness, and nihilism, which is called objective anxiety, in that it comes from the policeman's internal threats to his code of morality, whereas objective anxiety results from external threats to his self-esteem. Superego anxiety causes distress every bit as powerful as objective anxiety, and the individual also uses defense mechanisms to keep it from becoming conscious. Reaction formation again seems to be the most frequently used mechanism for coping with superego anxiety. The policeman uses this defense by unconsciously denying that he gets pleasure from the work while consciously being aware only of his hatred for it. When asked how he feels about his job, the typical police officer will say that it is demoralizing and disgusting. If asked what he likes about the job, he will say the camaraderie with brother officers, the vacation time, and the pension. If pressed further and asked how he feels about the street, he might say something positive in a humorous way and quickly change the subject.

Reaction formation against superego anxiety results in an attitude that could be called "benign cynicism." Just as malignant cynicism was the outcome of defenses against objective anxiety, so, too, is this less toxic form of cynicism the result of the use of reaction formation against superego anxiety.

Benign cynicism is characterized by a belief that the job is unrewarding—it is just a job. It is an effort at minimizing the emotional importance of the work. There is no rush of pleasure, no excitement, no feeling of omnipotence and superiority—it is just a bad job with good benefits. In fact, when the policeman says his job is lousy but it has a good pension, he is trying to deny that the job is very gratifying, a real turn on, because if he acknowledges how pleasurable the work really is, he is being immoral, he is being seduced by the street.

In order to resist the street's immoral pleasure, the cop must see it as unrewarding and degrading. By rejecting the street's appeal the officer resists seduction and detaches himself from his emotional pleasure. As a result, his behavior appears to be based on feelings of indifference, condescension, and contempt not only for the public, but also for the job itself.

These men are most likely to describe themselves as hapless social garbagemen because that self-definition denies the "bad" pleasure they cannot acknowledge. The police officers who use malignant cynicism to cope with objective anxiety caused by feelings of pain, helplessness and nihilism tend to describe themselves as powerful and superior, while those cops who try to deflect superego anxiety caused by feelings of pleasure from the work are usually more self-effacing. They disparage their role as being insignificant and mundane. In this respect, their cynicism is more benign. One policeman described his job this way: "I am supposed to sweep human garbage out of the way so the public doesn't have to deal with them. But no matter how much you sweep, there's always more. That's what this job is really about."

This job description is totally lacking any conscious awareness of the emotionally gratifying aspects of the job, the sense of danger, and the feeling of being powerful and special. It reflects the underlying need to deny the "bad" pleasure the cop receives from the work and to avoid feeling guilty for wanting and getting pleasure from power and aggression.

There are some policemen whose defense against immoral pleasure does not work, and there are those who do not feel anxious at all about being turned on by the street. These men do not suffer from superego anxiety at all, but readily accept the pleasure without any concern about whether it is bad or not. They are the "Clean Beat" cops described by Bowan (1981) in Chapter 4. These men become addicted to the street. At the extreme, some see the job as the most gratifying part of their lives, perhaps the only gratifying part. These officers live for the street. They are restless and irritable when they are away from the street and comfortable and energized when they get back to it.

Reming (1988) found that officers with an extremely high number of self-initiated felony arrests had personality characteristics that were more similar to those of habitual criminals than to those of police officers with an average number of arrests. According to Reming,

> The profile of the supercop (and the habitual criminal)...
> is characterized by dispositions toward control, aggressiveness, vigilance, rebelliousness, high energy level, frankness in expression, intense personal relationships, high self-esteem, feelings of uniqueness, extraversion, sociability, jealousy, possessiveness of sexual partner, tendency not to change opinions easily, philandering, and a tendency to avoid blame. (1988, p. 166)

In short, the highly active street cop is very much like the career criminals he arrests. In a very real sense, he is as much a "street person" as is his law-breaking counterpart in that his self-concept and his pursuit of pleasure are centered on his experience in the street. We might say that the street did not rub off on him, but that the job permitted the "street" in him to come out.

The power of the street may become so great that the addicted officer may leave his conventional life and his family for a woman from the street. When asked what he thinks motivated him to leave his family and suburban home for a woman from the street, the cop will often say that he does not feel alive at home or appreciated by his wife, and that his new woman makes him feel alive and appreciated because she will do everything for him and make him feel that she lives for him. He also will say that the suburbs are dead while the beat's neighborhood is alive and exciting.

A former police officer describes the experience this way:

> He gets services without having to perform because he's a cop. He gets status, distinction, authority, and power. He also is introduced to women who give him sex and reverence without his having to do anything for it. It's quite a perfume—it's quite an intoxication.
>
> If he has inherited his lifestyle rather than having chosen it, when he is challenged by temptation and opportunities he becomes confused and resentful that he has been deprived of those opportunities.
>
> He sees his life as depriving and one of being incarcerated. He has all that dependency and responsibility at home. There were guys who had very limited social experience. The selection of women they had experience with was from their own ethnic group. You talk about Ulysses and the Sirens, I know a lot of guys assigned to the South Bronx who cashed in their chips for Latin women.

The officer's conscious awareness of the gratification he receives from being a street cop—action, power, being regarded as superior and sexually desirable—is that he is a man's man in the street. The work has allowed him to make real his unconscious childhood fantasy of masculine power, aggression, and sexuality, and the cop cannot or does not want to resist its attraction. Ultimately he cannot leave the street because he unconsciously feels it is the only place where he can feel such intense pleasure.

One is reminded of the character, Captain Colby, in the film, *Apocalypse Now*. Having been sent to kill Colonel Kurtz because he had been seduced by power and aggression, Colby joins Kurtz instead of killing him. In much the same way, the policeman who is seduced by the street after having been sent there to civilize it experiences an intense pleasure that is difficult to renounce.

The work-addicted policeman regards the street as the major and perhaps the only source of "narcissistic supplies" (Kohut, 1971) in that his self-esteem, indeed, his self-identity, is derived from the gratification he gets from being the most powerful and special man in the street. He is very similar to the work-addicted patients treated by Fisher (1983). As Fisher's patients came to recognize their unconscious needs,

> each came to appreciate the central role of their motiva-
> tion to feel "special" and "superior." They reported that
> an intense and pervasive sense of pleasure accompanied
> the notion of being special. This "high" became a preoc-
> cupation that they described as analogous to drug addic-
> tion. (1983, p. 43)

Fisher describes the cause of this "high" as the "illusion of grandiosity" because the state of feeling special is "unrealistic and objectively false" (p. 43). However, unlike Fisher's civilian patients, the police officer's special status and power in the street are very real. Consequently, the officer's grandiosity is not a purely intrapsychic state because his external environment continually validates his self-concept of being superior. If the civilian workaholic can be seduced by the gratification provided by the "illusion of grandiosity," the concrete validation of the policeman's grandiosity in the street can only be described as ultraseductive.

Of all his ambivalent experiences, the police officer's ambivalence toward the work is the most difficult one to cope with. This reaction ranges from hate brought on by the repeated assaults on his fundamental beliefs about human beings to a pleasure so intense he must deny its existence. It is this conflict about the work that most policemen must resolve, usually by themselves, because it goes to the core of their self-concept as men and as human beings.

Chapter 6

A Psychodynamic View
of Some Issues
in Police Work

There are certain controversial issues in police work that have generated some research and much discussion. This chapter seeks to examine these issues from a psychodynamic slant in the hope of providing another perspective to complement the existing sociological descriptions. What follows is an attempt to look at police stress, the stereotype of the dumb cop, the police personality, corruption, and brutality with an eye on unconscious motivation, conflict, and defense. The goal is to gain a better understanding of the impact of unconscious thoughts and feelings on the police officer's behavior in these various situations.

POLICE STRESS

One of the most talked about issues in police work during the last 15 years is "police stress." The job came to be seen as a highly stressful one that exacted a high emotional toll on its officers. That this view followed a period in which police officers were regarded by many as sadistic is probably more than coincidence. It illustrates the public's ambivalence oscillating between seeing the police as stupid storm troopers and society's suffering heroes.

Just what police stress really is and what the term really means remains a puzzle. In his review of the theoretical approaches to stress, Violanti (1981) shows that the definition of stress varies according to the theory used to describe it. Webb and Smith (1980), Terry (1981) and Malloy and Mays (1984) reviewed the literature on police stress and concluded that the evidence for the existence of special stressors in police work is inconclusive. They also concluded that the hypothesis that police work is more stressful than all other occupations is also not supported. Their conclusion is corroborated by Anson and Bloom (1988). Malloy and Mays (1984) advised researchers "to abandon the hypothesis that all police officers are highly stressed and that this stress causes an unusually high incidence of alcoholism, drug abuse, psychophysiological disorders, cardiovascular disease, suicide or family disruption" (1984, p. 209).

If stress is such a vague concept and if its usefulness in describing its effects is restricted to the theory used to define it, why is the idea of police stress not only popular but seemingly well accepted as an important topic for research? The answer may be that if police stress is defined as an occupational health issue, then aspects of the job could be identified and isolated as high stressors.

Factors such as high visibility to the public, departmental procedures, regulations and punishments, and alienation from the community could be studied for their impact on stress. These types of factors were regarded as unique to police work and therefore made police stress qualitatively different from stress in other occupations.

The occupational health view permits researchers to define stress in a way that lends itself to empirical study with scientific methodology. The landmark studies of occupational stress in police were conducted by Kroes, Margolies, and Hurrell (1974) and by Kroes (1976); another important work was the publication of a symposium on job stress in police officers edited by Kroes and Hurrell (1975). The first study administered questionnaires to police officers asking them to list the most stressful parts of their job. Analysis of their responses indicated that there were two principal sources of stress: threats to the officer's self-image and professional status from the courts, the police department, and the public, and the officer's isolation from the rest of the community.

Kroes's (1976) study also surveyed police officers for stressful aspects of their job and identified five primary stressors unique to police work. These five were the courts, the public's negative image of police, having one's values assaulted by dealing with undesirables, racial confrontations, and line of duty and crisis situations.

These studies are "clean" in that they identify and isolate specific variables described by police as stressful. It would seem that research methodology within the occupational health frame of reference had isolated the specific troublemakers, and that stress would be significantly lowered by removing them from the job.

Shortly after publication of his book, Kroes began to treat police officers who had been injured or had difficulty coping with the job. He published a second edition of his book in 1985 in which he added a number of important stressors based on his clinical experience. The new stressors were departmental pressure to go to college, the lack of opportunity for promotion, performance anxiety, emotional responses to traumatic events, and emotional reaction to personal injury.

The last three clinical stressors identified by Kroes muddy the clean research waters since they are not readily identifiable and measurable by research methodology. Even more important, unlike the other stressors, it is difficult to alleviate these stressors and impossible to prevent them. These emotional factors are, in my opinion, some of the real troublemakers, and the stressors identified from questionnaires are probably the result of the officers' defense against their underlying anxiety.

Furthermore, since Kroes was working primarily with injured or sick officers in disability cases, his patients were troubled most by these negative emotional stressors. Had he also treated police officers who were uninjured or healthy, my guess is that other stressors, such as anxiety over changes in personality, loss of intimacy with one's wife, and bringing the street home, may have emerged.

The organizational viewpoint of police stress is readily observed in *Job Stress and the Police Officer*, a symposium sponsored by the National Institute of Occupational Safety and Health and edited by Kroes and Hurrell (1975). Many of the speakers lay the problem of police stress at the door of the police department's structure and management style. They indicate that making the department less punitive and less hierarchical with respect to decision making would make the job far less stressful. This view is undoubtedly correct, up to a point. What many speakers do not address is that even the most professionalized, egalitarian police department could not remove the intrapsychic conflicts created by being in the street. As long as the street remains as emotionally powerful as it is now, reforms of organizational structure and management style will have very little impact on the officer's emotional conflicts and the stress they produce.

The point is that any attempt to understand stress in police officers that does not take into account the intense feelings of hate and pleasure caused by the job cannot completely account for the phenomenon. It is true that the organization and management style is a source of stress for cops. It is true that the criminal justice system, the public, racial hostility, and crises contribute to police stress. But ultimately stress is an emotional experience, and the policeman's emotional experience of the work will have a great deal to say about its stress-inducing qualities.

To understand stress in policemen we must understand the impact of ambivalent feelings directed at cops and experienced by the cops themselves. The psychodynamic view is that stress in police officers, and everyone else for that matter, is a by-product of conflict. When we have mixed feelings, particularly opposing ones, they struggle for dominance. This conflict is perceived unconsciously and sometimes consciously as anxiety.

The euphemistic term for anxiety, which is regarded by many as sounding too pathological, is stress. As the reader may have already guessed, the psychodynamic position is that stress is caused by conflict, and the most intense conflict is caused by simultaneous feelings of love and hate called ambivalence. Stratton's (1984) analysis seems the most comprehensive of the approaches to police stress. He categorizes stress into:

1. external stressors: the courts, the public's hostility, adverse government decisions, ineffective referral agencies, and ineffective communication among criminal justice agencies;
2. internal stressors: poor training, poor supervision, poor career development opportunities, an inadequate departmental system of reward and reinforcement, offensive departmental policies, excessive paperwork, poor equipment, and arbitrary termination;
3. the work itself: role conflict, shift work, danger, the absence of closure in a case, constantly seeing people in pain, the responsibility for other people's safety, and having to accept the consequences of one's actions; and
4. personal stressors: incompetence, fear, being a nonconformist in the police peer group, being a female and/or ethnic minority, and "personal problems."

Yet, even Stratton's system does not directly address the officer's ambivalence toward those aspects of the work that cause him stress, nor does it take into account the capacity of the work to make him feel powerless and omnipotent. Stratton does allude to the emotional power of the work itself when he discusses "workaholism" and the "exhaustion syndrome."

> The workaholism stressor occurs when we combine dedication and excitement with the challenging aspects of police work, [and] they become addicting. The satisfying feeling of solving crimes or apprehending criminals, eliminating menaces from the community and preventing crimes, become the sole goals for many in these circumstances. The growing isolation from other events around them, the feeling that they can truly be "themselves" only around their colleagues, and perhaps also alienation from their families and spouses, can add to the vicious circle. (1984, p. 138)

Clearly, the workaholic cop is in love with his job; he does not love his job, he is in love with it. Why does this happen? Stratton does not go beyond describing the syndrome, nor does anyone else who studies stress in police officers. The psychodynamic explanation for the policeman falling for "la puta" is that the work gratifies his unconscious desire for power, for mastery over danger, and for the sexual gratification of being "the man."

When Stratton speaks of the officer's feeling that he can be "himself" only on the job, we must infer that the job allows him to satisfy his unconscious desires and to make his unconscious fantasies real, so that his ego ideal becomes real on the street and nowhere else. It is as if what is wished for in a daydream actually comes true. This is an incredibly powerful capacity of the job. In fact, given the ability of the work to gratify powerful wishes and fantasies, it is surprising that more policemen do not become addicted to the job.

Gilmartin (1986) suggests that one reason "cop work gets in the blood" (p. 445) is that the policeman is in a constant state of hypervigilance—being on the alert for danger and crime—while at work. Being hypervigilant, says Gilmartin, puts the autonomic nervous system in overdrive, which causes the officer to feel energized and vital, a state he finds pleasurable. In a real sense the cop is "turned on" by the work, even when he is engaged in routine patrol activities.

According to the psychodynamic view of workaholism, the addicted officer's response to satisfying his "primitive" desires and fantasies of omnipotence may be to give into the gratification without regard for the consequences to himself and his family. He cannot deny himself the intense pleasure of the street. His superego is not strong enough to keep his desires in check. The overwhelming of one's superego is an enormously anxiety-provoking experience because the individual is rejecting all the social and moral regulations that make one civilized.

Even though the officer may give in to his "bad" desires and reject the social and moral restrictions against pursuing bad pleasures, he is nonetheless in a state of extreme conflict because the superego, although overwhelmed at his conscious level, keeps struggling against his surrender at his unconscious level of experience. This conflict produces a significant degree of superego anxiety that the policeman tries to ward off by more vigorously pursuing bad pleasure to silence the superego. This vicious cycle often results in physical and emotional exhaustion—the burnout phenomenon described by Fisher (1983) in Chapter 5.

For the officer whose superego is strong enough to resist the power of bad pleasure, superego anxiety is also very strong. However, here the cop copes with superego anxiety by denying the bad pleasure of the job through the mechanism of reaction formation. In this case, the officer's conscious experience is that the job provides him with no gratification at all. This is the "benign" form of cynicism described in Chapter 5.

The cop consciously believes the job is without pleasure while he unconsciously derives considerable gratification from it. This is a compromise in which the superego gets something, namely, the conscious experience of not gaining bad pleasure, while the unconscious desire for pleasure also gets its share. It is this compromise that makes this form of police cynicism "benign." He can do his job, get pleasure from it, and feel that he is following his conscience. The price tag for this compromise is that he cannot allow himself to *consciously* derive pleasure from the work, so he sees the job as demoralizing and worthless—the social garbageman's perspective. This is a very stressful state to be in for 20 years—feeling that the job "sucks" every tour of every week for the cop's career. It is no wonder than that "police stress" is often defined as policemen hating their job.

As bad as this form of stress may be, it is far less toxic than the helplessness and pain the officer experiences when his value system is attacked by the brutality and degradation of the street. These experiences result in a great deal of objective anxiety. He copes with the objective anxiety by denying compassion for victims and by using reaction formation to deny feelings of helplessness. These defense mechanisms lead to attitudes and behavior that have been described as malignant cynicism.

The problem with the use of both benign and malignant cynicism is that the officer must deny any capacity to feel positive emotions as well as any feelings of vulnerability. The fact that the cop has quarantined his compassion and needs for intimacy and love does not mean that they have no impact on him. What happens is that these emotions and needs keep banging on the cell door to get out, causing him to feel conflict. He has to work extremely hard to keep these human attributes isolated, so that maintaining cynical attitudes and behavior becomes grueling work. I believe that the high emotional and physical cost of maintaining this defense is what Stratton is describing as the "exhaustion syndrome."

To sum up, the psychodynamic view of police stress is that it is the result of the policeman's emotional conflicts. One part of his conflict results from feeling overwhelmed by a cruel, uncivilized environment that is too powerful for him to master. The result is feelings of objective anxiety. The second part results from being gratified by the work in ways that threaten his moral code. He is deriving immoral pleasure that threatens to make *him* uncivilized and cruel. This conflict leads to superego anxiety. These two forms of anxiety—objective and superego—are at the heart of what is described as police stress. The police officer's stress is really his feelings of distress trying to cope with anxiety.

The idea that police stress has to do with unconscious conflicts and defense mechanisms is not a popular position. In fact, other than Symonds (1972, 1973), I did not find any direct statement concerning the role of unconscious forces in a police officer's experience. There are three reasons why this position is ignored. First, research designs do not apply very well to explorations of the unconscious. Consequently, a scientific approach to police stress would be extremely difficult to conduct if it had to isolate and measure unconscious factors.

The second reason is that the idea of unconscious motivation, conflict, and anxiety does not sit well with the police community. Neither police department administrators nor police officers themselves like the prospect of having cops "analyzed." Such an approach hints at pathology and instability among police, so high-level police officials would be reluctant at best to have their personnel "shrunk" even by pen-and-paper surveys. In addition, the police subculture is hostile to considering the role of unconscious forces in police behavior because it threatens the subculture's self-definition as just a group of simple men who like to work outdoors and to help society. Jacobi (1975) believes that "emotionality and emotional disturbance are anathema in the police culture" (p. 93). Acknowledging emotional distress thus invites administrative sanctions by the department and ostracism by peers. It also threatens the subculture's sociopolitical power. If police officers were thought of as having internal conflicts and anxieties, then they would not be regarded as powerful and superior to the civilian population. The police mystique of being special and different from civilians would be undermined.

The third reason is that the psychodynamic view of police stress does not lend itself to coming up with simple solutions to the problem. The occupational health and organizational management approaches can conduct scientific research, collect and analyze data, and formulate recommendations to alleviate police stress. Studies can lead to straightforward changes such as eliminating rotating shifts, buying better radios, giving sergeants training in leadership, and other specific stress-reducing strategies. However, the psychodynamic view says the problem is much more complex and less susceptible to simple solutions. The problem of police stress has to do with human nature rather than departmental procedures and organization. And human nature is very resistant to change of any kind.

THE "DUMB" COP

One of the most prevalent images of the policeman is that he is stupid. In Chapter 2, the public's ambivalent feelings toward the police officer were reflected in the portrayal of the cop as omnipotent, benevolent parent or incompetent, malevolent parent. The perception of the policeman as stupid is intimately connected with the unconscious belief that if he cannot help, it is because he is too stupid or too cruel to help.

Victims of crime frequently disparage the uniformed police officer who is first on the scene for being too dumb to understand what has happened. This attitude results from the victim's unconscious wish that the all-powerful cop will catch the criminal, return the victim's property, heal the victim's injury, and restore his or her self-esteem, conflicting with the reality of the cop's behavior.

Instead of jumping in his patrol car to catch the criminal, the cop asks mundane questions about details of the crime; instead of bringing back the stolen property, he asks for an inventory and an estimate of the value of the stolen property; instead of providing immediate first aid to heal the victim's injury, the officer asks if the victim wants to go to the emergency room; and instead of taking away the victim's fear of being vulnerable, he gives perfunctory words of advice about being more aware and trying to take commonsense preventive steps.

When the victim does not get rescued by the police officer, his or her emotional reaction is that even though policemen are trained to be all-powerful, it is obvious that *this* one is too stupid to apply what he has learned. He is too dumb to realize what has transpired, and too dumb to recognize that all he needs to do is use his power to make everything right again. It is not surprising that by the end of the cop's interviewing of the victim, he is subjected to hostility and contempt for being competent only to ask questions and write the answers in his notebook. When he leaves, the victim may be more furious at him for being more a miserable failure than a strong, protective parent than the victim is at the criminal.

In this all too familiar scenario, the victim's unconscious wish for total security to be given by the police officer is, of course, very unrealistic. However, being victimized, that is, made to feel powerless and humiliated by the criminal, causes the victim to rely on regression to ward off feeling helpless. Regression is defined as an "ego defense mechanism in which the individual retreats to the use of less mature responses in attempting to cope with stress and maintain ego integrity" (Coleman, 1964, p. 669). In using regression, the victim relies on seeing and reacting in ways that were helpful in the past to preserve his or her ego from being overwhelmed. So, the victim begins to see things through a younger person's eyes and to act as a younger person would to avoid feeling helpless. The problem is that the regressed victim feels like a kid and sees the cop as a powerful, loving daddy.

Not surprisingly, when the cop does not behave like the daddy the victim expects, the victim feels unfairly deprived and becomes angry at the cop for being such a miserable excuse for the strong father who can make everything all right again. From the victim's point of view, this daddy is obviously a defective one—he is too stupid to know how to make everything better. If the cop-daddy was smart enough to do what he was capable of, then he could make everything as it was before the crime. However, this one cannot, so he must be dumb.

This description of the victim's unconscious wishes, the depriving reality of the policeman's behavior, and the victim's subsequent anger toward him have an effect on the officer. The victim is not the only one feeling helpless; the policeman also knows that there is little he can do to make everything better, and anything that can be done will be the job of the detectives, if they decide to follow through on this case. Like the victim, the policeman relies on a defense mechanism to keep from feeling overwhelmed by powerlessness. As described in Chapter 5, he often relies on denial to ward off feelings of compassion because they will only heighten his feeling helpless to do anything for the victim. Consequently, his unemotional, businesslike demeanor comes across to the victim as a lack of awareness of the victim's distress and needs. His "just the facts ma'am" behavior is interpreted as his lack of understanding of the seriousness of the victim's plight and of what he can and should do to alleviate it. Put simply, he is too stupid to know what has happened and what to do about it.

The officer's demeanor serves to confirm the victim's reaction that this cop does not know what the hell is going on. All he can do is ask stupid questions that are useless in catching the bad guy. Furthermore, he is not even emotionally involved, so he must not know how bad things are. Unhappily for both parties, a vicious cycle is established in which the victim's increasing anger toward the officer is met by still more detachment, so that in the end there is no longer an officer assisting a victim, there is a dumb cop coping with an ungrateful, demanding asshole. No wonder then that the victim believes the cop is stupid.

A second cause of the dumb cop image stems from the issuing of a warning or a summons. When a policeman uses his authority to restrict or punish a civilian's behavior, the civilian is made to feel helpless in the face of the officer's power. Since everyone's ego spends a great deal of energy protecting itself from feeling helpless, the civilian's ego defends itself by relying on rationalization as a defense. Rationalization is a mechanism "in which the individual thinks up 'good' reasons to justify what he has done, is doing, or intends to do" (Coleman, 1964, p. 669).

When issued a warning or summons, the civilian will react by thinking that his or her violation was so insignificant that any intelligent person would ignore it. But since this cop is making a big deal over something so small, he must not be smart enough to know when something is important or not. The civilian then thinks, "If this cop is chasing me around for practically nothing and there are people being murdered and robbed in the streets, he must be too dumb to know which offense is more important."

If the civilian should say something to that effect to the officer, the policeman will feel threatened and rely on a defense mechanism to cope with it. If the civilian is lucky, the officer will rely on denial by believing he is totally unaffected by the civilian's hostility. The policeman's indifference will be perceived by the civilian as a failure to understand the explanation for the infraction, thus proving the cop is dumb. If the civilian is unlucky, the officer will rely on aggression instead of a defense mechanism, with the result that the civilian gets verbal abuse, another summons, or both. The civilian may even be arrested if he or she tries to meet the officer's counterattack. In this case, the officer's abuse is perceived by the civilian as proof of the cop's stupidity for responding to an "innocent explanation" (once again, rationalization is used) by becoming abusive and threatening more undeserved punishment. Whether the officer is apathetic or aggressive in responding to the civilian, the consequence will be that he is seen as stupid.

In addition to the belief among victims and violators that policemen are dumb, there is a prevailing social attitude that also regards policemen as mental incompetents. In fact, early studies of intelligence in police officers (Terman *et al.*, 1917;

Thurstone, 1922) indicated that they scored well below average on intelligence tests. Later studies (Matarazzo, 1964; McManus *et al.*, 1970; Fenster & Locke, 1973) found that officers' IQ scores were average or above average. It is quite likely that the public perception of police as dumb has little to do with the officers' intellectual abilities. Rather, it has more to do with unconscious issues regarding power and aggression.

Since the police officer has the legal power to regulate and punish the behavior of civilians, then civilians will of necessity feel powerless in comparison to him. As I have been saying with the frequency of a broken record, this unequal relationship recapitulates the civilian's childhood relationship with his or her parents, the only other people who have had the right to regulate and punish his or her behavior. How can the civilian maintain self-esteem and a sense of being equal to the policeman without actually challenging his power and being made to feel like a helpless child?

One way is to use rationalization to explain away the inequality in the relationship by saying that power and intelligence are mutually exclusive attributes: if you have one, you cannot have the other. "So," concludes the civilian, "if the cop has the power (read that as brawn), I must have the brains." My impression is that this defense is used quite often when it is clear that some people have more power or strength than the rest of us. Athletes in sports requiring great strength are stereotyped as stupid. The average male sees them as pea-brained behemoths in order to be compensated for his relative weakness by feeling smarter. In the same way, the civilian also feels compensated and regards himself as having the brains if the cop has the power. His perceived greater intelligence evens out the relationship so that he has the intelligence the cop does not have, even though the cop has power that he does not have.

It seems to me that the stereotype of the dumb cop as defense against helplessness would not be as popular as it is if it did not receive reinforcement from the police subculture's rules of behavior. If the civilian wants to believe the policeman has power but no brains, the subculture seems to require the officer to act just that way—as a swaggering tough guy who acts first and thinks later.

The pressure of the peer group to demand specific behavior from its members is quite powerful. The "squad room rules of conduct" are to be followed to the letter if the policeman wishes to avoid ostracism. One very important prohibition is to deny emotions. Says Stratton,

> Feelings are rarely talked about among police officers. The new officer learns this quickly. By trying to imitate those they perceive as being successful on the job, the new cop may be denying a very important part of himself—his feelings. (1984, p. 85)

The policeman not only tries to deny his emotional reactions, he also presents himself as tough and powerful, in a real sense superior to the civilian victim or violator with whom he deals. The "tough cop" persona enables him to project any feelings of helplessness and vulnerability onto the victim and to maintain his authority over the violator-asshole.

Besides enabling the policeman to project feeling helpless, being tough is mandated by the policeman's peers who tell him in no uncertain terms that toughness is the only acceptable behavior, particularly in the street where he must be like "a soldier, and soldiers must always display strength and hide vulnerability.... Soldiering is the embodiment of courage, strength and toughness. To sustain these virtues, however, the soldier had to repress vulnerability, sensitivity, fear and compassion" (Trompetter, 1986). Like the soldier, the policeman's peers expect courage, toughness, and emotional detachment.

The problem with presenting one's self as tough and unemotional is that to the civilian victim such behavior looks very much like indifference at best and hostility at worst. To the violator the policeman's toughness makes him appear more like a bully than an authority.

Anyone who has been pushed around in the school playground by the class bully concludes that the bully is stupid for picking on him or her. In much the same way, the tough cop's demeanor when issuing a warning or summons must be experienced by the civilian as bullying. "This is not someone enforcing the law, this is a stupid bully picking on me instead of on someone his own size," concludes the civilian.

The origins of the "dumb cop" image are thus complex. The failure of the police officer to gratify the victim's unconscious wish that he be omnipotent and curative leads to the feeling that he is stupid. To the violators who rationalized that their infraction is so small that it does not warrant punishment, the cop who gives them a summons appears stupid. Finally, when a police officer appears apathetic instead of compassionate toward a victim or when an officer issues a summons with tough guy's style, he appears to be a stupid bully. The unconscious reactions of civilians and the police officer himself are the causes of the perception of the cop as dumb.

THE POLICE PERSONALITY

The Predispositional Personality

Many people say that the last job they would ever consider is being a cop. They quickly count off all the negative aspects of the job that make it totally unacceptable: there is the physical danger inherent in the work; there is the psychological danger of apathy and hostility from the public; there is the health risk of rotating shifts and being propelled from boredom to alarm every day, perhaps every hour; there is the damage to one's family and social life caused by being labeled as a police family; and there is the emotional toll of seeing human misery and degradation on a daily basis. With this laundry list of harmful results of being a policeman, civilians often ask, "Who would want to be a cop?"

The answer is that a lot of young men want to be a cop. Even with all the terrible things that inevitably go with the ' job, these men want to do police work and they want it badly. They are willing to take entrance examinations, have their past investigated, go through a rigorous and protracted training period during which they must demonstrate competence in a wide range of activities, and they must behave according to far more rigorous standards on and off duty than civilians do.

In fact many rejected applicants spend considerable amounts of time and money appealing their rejection to earn a second chance to become a policeman. "Since the job is so bad, there must be something about these men who want it that sets them apart from the rest of us," concludes the civilian.

Behavioral scientists have studied police applicants to determine whether there are particular personality patterns among them that differ from those of the civilian population. This area of research seeks to determine if there are personality factors that make an individual predisposed to be attracted to police work.

When an applicant is asked why he wants to be a police officer, he usually gives three reasons. The first is that he wants to do something to help society, to make the world a better place; the second is for the salary benefits and pension; and the third is that he likes variety and challenges (Reiser, 1973; Van Maanen, 1973; Arcuri, 1976; Lester, 1983; Slater & Reiser, 1988). When asked to expand on his third reason, the applicant usually says he expects to face many different problems and to rely on himself to solve them.

Let us look at the most popular reason given for wanting to be a police officer, namely, service to society. In my experience, police applicants and recruits do not regard themselves as wanting to be public servants. While public service is an important motive for choosing police work, the image conveyed in the term "helping people" is not so much serving as much as it is rescuing people. When these men speak of being of assistance to others, they mean using their power and strength to help the powerless and weak. Such an image has obvious elements of dominance and action rather than service in its traditional sense.

Lefkowitz (1977) has a similar view of the public service motive for choosing police work:

> Although police also appear to be motivated by social service considerations...the emphasis ought to be on *social* (working with others rather than autonomously) rather than on *service,* since the nature of the policeman's social relationships may involve a need to dominate rather than help others. (p. 347)

In this context the desire to help others is actually the by-product of the wish to be identified by himself and others as brave, powerful, and virtuous. My guess is that the candidate's desire to help others is more personally and socially acceptable to express than the less conscious wish to be a powerful hero. It is quite possible that altruism as a motive masks the strong "recognition hunger" suggested by Symonds (1972).

The second popular reason for choosing police work as a career is financial security. The job is viewed by the applicant as well paying, relatively free from the threat of layoffs, providing extensive health benefits, and, of course, the pension. This assessment is very accurate. However, from a psychodynamic point of view, something is missing, that something being the emotional underpinning of the need for security. It appears that men who seek to be police officers search simultaneously for recognition as powerful heroes and for protection by the police department as benevolent parent from feeling vulnerable and inadequate.

The juxtaposition of the wish for power and recognition and the desire for protection and security suggests that feelings of wanting power and autonomy exist simultaneously with dependent wishes for protection and security. If this is the case, then the young man's choice of police work becomes clarified. The job can satisfy both of these opposite wishes by giving him clearly identified and recognized power as well as security from feeling powerless and afraid.

This simultaneous pressure of power-autonomy needs and protection-security needs may explain why police officers express the desires for strict, directive supervisors and also to do their job without supervision. These opposite wishes suggest what Lefkowitz calls "ambivalences along the assertiveness-dependency continuum" (1977, p. 350). Policemen may have strong needs at both ends of the continuum that cause them to have opposing feelings about how much independence and direction they want while on the job. Ambivalence resulting from autonomy and dependency needs may also support Symond's suggestion that police welcome a tough commissioner because they cannot stand feeling compliant to a soft-spoken boss (1972, p. 168). To comply with "soft supervision" means to depend on a weak and inadequate parent. To work with no supervision at all may lead to feelings of vulnerability and weakness, given the officer's need for protection and security by the department. While this hypothesis may be speculative, I believe it focuses attention on the unconscious and often conflicting desires of men who look to police work as a way of gratifying these opposite desires for power and nurturance.

The third popular reason given by the typical applicant for wanting to be police officers is the wish to be challenged by a variety of problems and to solve them on his own. When pressed to be more specific, he says he expects to be in dangerous situations and to be brave and smart enough to handle them. It seems that the underlying meaning of "variety and challenge" is mastering danger. "The risky aspect of the profession, the element of personal danger," says Stratton, "tends to be seen as exciting rather than as a deterrent to entering police work. Those drawn toward police careers tend to be action-oriented" (1984, p. 33). The applicant is looking for excitement, for "unforeseen action," as Stratton puts it (1984, p. 34).

In short, he seeks the thrill of mastering danger, of experiencing himself as both brave and powerful. This motive has been labeled as "crime fighting" (Golden, 1982) and "power and status" (Lester, 1983). These labels connote conscious wishes. My impression is that unconscious wishes might be labeled "omnipotent heroism." Evidence for the wish for omnipotent heroism is not statistical, but it is empirical nonetheless. For example, police academy instructors say that they have two main training goals. The first is to make recruits alert to danger and the second is to get them to stop wanting to be heroes. The wish to be heroic is described as jumping into dangerous situations without proper backup and seeing nonthreatening situations as dangerous and then overreacting.

Instructors usually believe the wish to see danger in every situation results from watching television cop shows, but as discussed in Chapter 2 the cop shows feed an already existing set of fantasies of policemen and their work that makes the job so attractive to recruits.

Another example is the policy of many departments to put rookie police officers under close supervision during their probation period. The department's rationale is twofold: the first is to observe the rookie's performance; the second is to keep him from making minor incidents into major ones or jumping headlong into danger without taking proper precautions. In essence, the departments are trying to "cool off" their rookies by keeping their fantasies on a tight leash.

At first glance, the unconscious desire to be an all-powerful hero sounds abnormal. Any man whose underlying wish to be a policeman is based on the pleasure of mastering danger by using power sounds like a terrible prospect. However, psychological testing of applicants reveals that the personality profiles of those who are accepted as recruits are within the normal range. Whether the instrument is a personality inventory such as the Minnesota Multiphasic Personality Inventory (Gottesman, 1969; Balch, 1972; Saccuzzo et al., 1974; Saxe & Reiser, 1976; Bartol, 1982; Klopsch, 1983; Carpenter & Raza, 1987), the California Psychological Inventory (Bianchi, 1973; Hogan and Kurtines, 1975; Mills & Bohannon, 1980) or the Sixteen Personality Factors (Cattell *et al.*, 1970; Topp & Kurdash, 1986), the personality profiles of accepted applicants are within the normal range. The term "normal" in this case refers to the clinical rather than statistical meaning.

If these men who unconsciously strive to feel they are all-powerful heroes are not abnormal, then what makes them different from men who do not wish to be police officers? Perhaps it is not that police candidates have this desire and others do not, but that all men have this unconscious wish. Perhaps the difference is one of how much they have this wish rather than whether they have it at all. It seems likely that almost every man has the unconscious wish to be a hero, but that the police candidate has more of it. While men who choose to remain civilians settle for the vicarious experience of being powerful and brave by imagining they are the cops they see on television, those who choose to be cops feel the need to make the wish a reality.

Some support for this hypothesis comes from Gottesman (1969) who administered the Minnesota Multiphasic Personality Inventory (MMPI) to police applicants and found, as did other investigators, that this group had elevated K-scale scores. A high K score indicates the subject is trying to fake "looking good" by trying to answer in a way that presents him in a favorable light. Gottesman points out that even after becoming cops, these men with elevated K scores continue to have high K scores despite the fact that they are already in the police department. He says,

> elevation of K scores to the level noted is indicative of defensiveness, pretensions of invulnerability and attempts to maintain a facade of imperturbability. These characteristics appear to be important and persistent characteristics of those men who gravitate into police work and remain in the field.... It is quite conceivable in the police context... that such defensiveness and pretensions are part of the applicant's "self-concept" and, as such, are necessary characteristics for successful performance of police duties. (1969, p. 135)

Gottesman is suggesting that the applicant may be expressing his view of who he is rather than merely as a conscious attempt to appear favorable. This means that the applicant unconsciously wants to appear invulnerable and imperturbable to himself as well as consciously to convince the police department to accept him. To a man who wishes to see himself as invulnerable (omnipotent) and imperturbable (unafraid), police work is a way to validate this self-concept. Therefore, what may differentiate the civilian from the potential policeman is that the civilian is satisfied fantasizing and pretending to be omnipotent and brave, while the police candidate needs to consciously experience himself that way in the real world.

Shev (1977) offers a psychoanalytic hypothesis of the male's motivation to be a policeman that centers about the young boy's Oedipal wish to rescue his mother from his father. This "rescue fantasy," suggests Shev, becomes the stimulus for the individual to choose police work as a way of satisfying the need to protect his mother from his father. In rescuing victims from perpetrators, he will gratify the desire to rescue his mother from his bad father. Shev bases his hypothesis on the high percentage of police officers who come from overtly broken homes or from families in which the father or both parents were emotionally if not physically absent.

Although the rescue fantasy may be the underlying motive for some men to select police work as a career, it would be an overgeneralization to conclude that it is the principal motive in all police candidates. Certainly every applicant does not come from an overtly or covertly broken home. Furthermore, there are many young men from broken homes and dysfunctional families who do not wish to be policemen, nor do they seek occupations in which rescuing others is either a concrete or symbolic component of the work. A generalization that can be made, I believe, is that the desire to master dangerous situations in order to demonstrate one's bravery and power appears to be the primary motive for men to want to be police officers.

The Occupational Personality

While the predispositional personality approach to study-
ing police officers suggests cops are born and not made, the
occupational view maintains that a policeman's personality is
produced by his experiences once he is on the job. This view
believes that the work makes permanent changes in the
officer's personality structure that prior to his becoming a cop
was very much a typical civilian personality (Dodd, 1967;
Niederhoffer, 1967; Black, 1968; Wilson, 1968). They maintain
that the job of police officer causes men to change their personality. They acquire traits such as "authoritarianism, suspiciousness, physical courage, cynicism, loyalty, secretiveness,
conservatism, loyalty, secretiveness, and self-assertiveness"
(Lefkowitz, 1975, p. 6). Implicit in this position is that the
work taints good men and changes them for the worse. If this
sounds familiar, it is because it corroborates the policeman's
own negative feeling (as discussed in Chapter 4) that constant
exposure to misery and degradation has caused him irrepa-
rable emotional harm.

The research literature on the police occupational personality has been contradictory. Those studies which have used
self-report inventories as measures of personality appear to
detect a cluster of attributes that support the idea that the
policeman's self-concept is intimately connected with the need
to feel masculine, powerful, and brave. For example, studies
using the Edwards Personal Preference Schedule (EPPS) found
that policemen score higher than the norm on needs for
achievement, exhibition, and heterosexuality and lower on
needs for affiliation, abasement, nurturance, and order (Sterling, 1972; Simon et al., 1973; Sheppard et al., 1974; Butler &
Cochrane, 1977; Lester et al., 1980).

When the MMPI was used, the results were more equiv-
ocal. Klopsch (1983) found that group scale scores of police
officers on the MMPI remained stable after five years on the
job, but that there was considerable individual variation between pre- and posttest scale scores. Thus police work did not
have a uniform impact on the officers; otherwise the individ-

ual variation in scores would have been in the same direction rather than in a random fashion. Klopsch's findings did not support the occupational personality hypothesis. Fenster and Locke (1973) found that noncollege-educated policemen had significantly higher masculinity subscale scores on the MMPI than did civilians.

Another personality inventory used in the study of police officers is the California Personality Inventory (CPI). Research using the CPI has found that highly rated police officers score higher on dominance and self-control scales (Mills & Bohannon, 1980), capacity for status (Pugh, 1985), and intellectual efficiency, self-confidence, and sociability (Hogan, 1971; Hogan & Kurtines, 1975). Police officers receiving high ratings by supervisors also scored high on the Sixteen Personality Factor Questionnaire scales that indicate tough-minded and aggressive personality attributes (Fabricatore *et al.*, 1978). However, since these studies are concerned only with police officers receiving high supervisory ratings, they do not provide any evidence for the existence of any global impact of the job on the personalities of all officers, both highly rated and otherwise.

If we examine the results of these various studies of personality profiles of police officers, a few qualities seem to consistently emerge. First, policemen see themselves as needing to be tough, strong, and brave. Second, they see themselves as being dominant, that is, having power. It seems that in a real sense the police officer has become the man he wanted to be when he chose to be a policeman. This actualized self-concept may be the underlying factor in the debate over the policeman's "working personality."

Thus what may set the cop apart from the civilian is his opportunity to actualize his unconscious wishes through the reality of his job, an opportunity few civilians may have. If this is the case, then the job does *make* the man, but it does not *create* him. The job permits fantasies to become real. In the street the policeman really is more powerful than civilians, he is required to conquer his fear and to master danger, he is self-reliant, tough, and resourceful. He has become the man he always dreamed of being.

The impact of such a gratifying experience must of necessity affect a man's personality. He must see himself differently in light of the significant and unique person he has become; he must regard himself as a man's man. If there is an occupational personality among policemen, I believe it has to do with his emphasis on using power and bravery to define himself. Having said that, I do not suggest that all policemen cope with their enhanced view of themselves in the same way. Many policemen become more tolerant of the weakness of others, while many become contemptuous of the weaker civilian world. Some become kinder and discover the depth of their humanity, while others become cruel and lose any recognition of their membership in the civilian world.

Since the reactions of policemen to becoming the man of their fantasies varies according to the unique makeup of each man, the personality changes caused by these reactions will also he highly individualized rather than universal. Therefore, like Klopsch's MMPI profiles of policemen, there must be changes in a man's personality caused by police work, but the nature and extent of the changes are going to depend on each man's psychological makeup.

POLICE CORRUPTION

The Public

Corruption in the police department almost always leads to a visceral response from the public. Unlike its more blasé reactions to revelations of wrongdoing by other public officials, society's response to police misconduct is invariably characterized by shock and an outcry for reform of the entire department. Crooked politicians, lawyers, and judges have not caused shock and demands for overhauling the electoral process or the legal system, so why is the public's reaction to crooked cops much more intense?

One reason may lie in the public's unconscious wish to see the policeman as all-perfect, benevolent parent who can do no wrong. Having given the policeman the parental power to protect it, the public wants him to be the omnipotent, benevolent father whose only wish is to care for his children. As described in Chapter 2, the desire for the police officer to be a loving parent causes the civilian to see him as heroic not only in strength but also in virtue. Not only can he do no wrong, he is motivated only to do right. Unconsciously the civilian wants the policeman's power to be a source of protection and nurturance.

When the police officer abuses his power for personal gain, the civilian feels betrayed by this parent who is neither heroic nor virtuous, but who is instead a malevolent parent whose aim is to gratify himself at the civilian's expense. At this point the idealization of the officer as good parent is replaced by considerable hate for him as bad parent, and what typically follows is a collective rage response by the public to punish this cruel and dangerous parent. At this point the underlying ambivalence felt by the public for the policeman is most apparent. Love quickly turns to hate when the loving good parent transforms himself into the cruel, sadistic adult who uses his power to harm rather than help his children.

Consequently, the public's emotional response to the discovery of bad cops is due to its unconscious ambivalent feelings toward the cop as parent. The public does not have such intense ambivalent emotions toward other public officials because they do not possess the parental power to physically protect or punish the civilian.

The Department

The police department usually tries to deal with corruption by employing the "rotten apple" explanation (Knapp Commission, 1980). Essentially the "rotten apple" view says that the vast majority of cops are in fact completely honest, but that a tiny minority of corrupt applicants managed to get through the screening process to become officers. It is this small group that is responsible for betraying the public trust and tarnishing the reputation of the honest police officers.

The department's view serves two important purposes. First, it preserves the public's unconscious wish for police to be omnipotent, virtuous heroes. In effect the department is saying that its men are indeed the benevolent parents the public wants them to be. The few bad apples are the rare exceptions to the honest, heroic men in the department. Second, by maintaining that only a few deviants cannot live up to the standards of behavior set for its officers, the department seeks to preserve its perfectionistic and often contradictory regulations for police conduct. The demand that a police officer's behavior be exemplary both on and off duty, that he follow correct procedure when there may be several "correct" procedures for a particular situation, or even no procedures at all, permits the department to say that one can realistically expect its officers to handle every situation correctly because they have been trained to do so.

Consequently, the department never has to examine its own involvement in contributing to the dilemma of corruption among its individual officers. By justifying its perfectionistic demands of the officer as realistic, the department deflects public criticism from itself to the "bad apples." The result, as former NYPD Commissioner Patrick V. Murphy (1973) says, is that the department can blame the rotten apples when it is the barrel that requires scrutiny. In essence the department's strategy is a kind of organizational defense mechanism. Declaring that its cops are and should be totally virtuous enables the department to ward off anxiety caused by public attack by displacing the public's hostility onto the police officers.

Much of the literature on police corruption focuses on the impact of peer pressure on the policeman to become corrupt (Stoddard, 1968; Bahn, 1975; Barker, 1976). Since membership in the police fraternity is vitally important to every officer, the requirement for membership may include participating in the group's corrupt activities. This viewpoint says that if his peers are corrupt, the cop will of necessity be forced to become corrupt if he wants to be accepted by his brother officers. Due to his isolation from the rest of society, so this thesis goes, the officer needs the police subculture to gain a sense of his identity and the feeling of belonging to a reference group that supports and protects him.

No one can argue that the officer's peer group is of great importance to him or that he feels enormous pressure to conform to its demands, whether to be tough and aggressive or to be corrupt. However, this approach does not provide any understanding of the causes of corruption among the peer group. It does not tell us why a sufficient number of policemen become corrupt in the first place to make corrupt behavior a subcultural requirement for all its members. To understand the rules of the peer group, we must first try to come to grips with the underlying psychological forces within each of its individual members.

The Police Officer

In describing the nature and extent of corruption in the New York Police Department, the Knapp Commission (1980) distinguished two types of corrupt police officers: the "grass eaters" and the "meat eaters." The meat eaters are

> those policemen who...aggressively misuse their police power for personal gain.... Although the "meat eaters" get huge payoffs that make the headlines, they represent a small percentage of all corrupt policemen. (p. 263)

On the other hand, the "grass eaters" are those police who

> simply accept the payoffs that the happenstances of policework throw their way.... The truth is, the vast majority of policemen on the take don't deal in huge amounts of graft. And yet, grass eaters are the heart of

the problem. Their great numbers tend to make corruption "respectable." (p. 263)

The acknowledgment that police corruption is widespread and for relatively small amounts of money suggests a number of things. First, the vast majority of officers are exposed to bribery of one sort or another during the course of their day-to-day work, and a large percentage of them accept bribes for small sums of money. Second, most police who accept bribes do not go looking for them—bribes are offered to them because of their power over the civilian with the money in his or her hand. Third, there is the belief among police that taking bribes is perfectly acceptable despite the department's pronouncements to the contrary. These three conclusions suggest that there is something emotionally significant about the offer of a bribe to the cop—something that has more to do with emotional rather than financial reward.

The reality that just being a cop makes an enormous number of civilians his supplicants, that these civilian supplicants wish to offer him tribute in recognition of his power over them, and that accepting these tributes is perfectly acceptable because they confirm his special status in society makes the emotional significance of the bribe far more important than just the opportunity to pocket a few more dollars as "fringe benefits." Niederhoffer's (1967) observation is particularly appropriate here:

> In performing his special role in the social system, the policeman realizes that for much of his time on duty he is above the law.... This sense of power often corrupts him into a belief that he is above the law. (p. 92)

Schlossberg (1974) and Rubinstein (1973) suggest that the gratuity or small bribe connotes the police officer's inferior social status. They say that the gratuity-bribe is really a tip for extra service from a servant, so that the money actually reinforces the cop's role as servant and identifies him as a member of the working class.

I believe this explanation of grass eating is itself a defense against acknowledging the bad pleasure of feeling superior. It is a reaction formation in that the cop who consciously feels like a servant receiving a tip is denying the unacceptable unconscious feeling of pleasure at being superior. If policemen truly felt that accepting free meals or clothes or taking money made him feel inferior to the civilian making the offer, then small-time corruption would be far less a problem than it is. It is precisely because these offers permit him to feel that his superiority is being acknowledged that grass eating is so pervasive.

The position that small-time corruption provides big-time emotional satisfaction is supported by the work of Aultman (1976). Using role theory as his reference, Aultman suggests that the policeman seeks to validate his special status and power when he accepts a bribe. He labels this attempt to demonstrate his superior position as "role-expressive" behavior:

> It is suggested that in some instances the police officer may resort to acceptance of gratuities or bribes in an attempt to validate a claim to authority. By demonstrating such position of control, officers may feel that they are expressing their role of authority by behaving in a manner that affirms an occupationally powerful position. (1976, p. 328)

Therefore, accepting a bribe validates the officer's special status because his power is recognized by the civilian supplicant. While Aultman's view has to do with the desire to express one's role rather than with the pursuit of emotional gratification, I believe the role theory and psychodynamic perspectives are complementary in that the former is an externally oriented approach while the latter is focused on the unconscious, internal experiences of the policeman.

Taking the concept of role-expressive behavior and putting it into psychodynamic terms, when a police officer accepts free meals, clothing, liquor, or big discounts on expensive items, he is gratifying his need to be special. When

he shows his shield and receives special privileges, he is getting more than a financial bargain: he is obtaining the pleasure
of having his special status validated by the merchant. "Flashing the tin" is thus a source of real emotional pleasure. Anyone
who has gone straight to the front of a long line at a restaurant
or who received a free item because the store owner was a
friend knows the intense feeling of pleasure the policeman
feels on a regular basis simply by flashing the tin.

It is unrealistic at best and folly at worst for the police
department or the public to demand that the cop deprive himself of the very real emotional pleasure of feeling special by
requiring him to refuse a gratuity or to expect that he will
never accept a small bribe. This is not to say that such behavior should be condoned. I am simply saying that the public
and the police cannot expect moral perfection from the police
because human beings are pleasure-seeking creatures who
have trouble resisting pleasure for virtue.

Consequently, the citizenry and the department cannot
afford to react with indignation and outrage when a cop reveals himself to be less than morally perfect. Corrupt policemen should be punished, of course, but the punishment
should fit the offense. The demand that the officer be morally
perfect or else a pariah is more a reflection of our unconscious
love of him as the all-good, loving parent or our hatred of
him as the malevolent, incompetent parent when he fails to
be perfect.

Until now we have been describing the prevalence of
"grass eaters" in police work for whom accepting gratuities
or small bribes is an affirmation of their superior status and
power which provides considerable pleasure. Let us now examine the "meat eaters," who are very different individuals
from their grass-eating counterparts. When it comes to receiving payoffs from criminals to look the other way, or stealing
money from perpetrators, or stealing drugs from pushers and
selling them from the back of a police car, then we are talking
about something more than the pleasure of feeling special.
What the meat eater wants is the basic pleasure that comes

from the use of raw power and the feeling of omnipotence that results from feeling immune from not only the legislated rules of behavior but the moral ones as well.

The meat eater has surrendered to the pleasure of doing whatever he wants and to the rush that comes from feeling powerful enough to have no restraints from the law and from his conscience. He has given in to his unconscious desire to be free of societal prohibitions and his own conscience. In effect, the meat eater does not experience superego anxiety that results from feeling one has violated the rules of one's conscience for wanting bad pleasure. He has given in to the rules of the street where gratifying one's desires is the only rule to be observed. He does not need to rely on cynicism because he does not need to defend himself from superego anxiety. Instead, the meat eater is always energized to make the big score, to haul in the big bucks. He is far from cynical about his job because police work is no longer upholding the law, it is the exercise of power to gratify his impulses.

Shealy (1977) believes that corrupt cops are born, not made, and his research suggests that it is possible to identify applicants who are more likely to become corrupt policemen. If Shealy is correct, then it is likely that he can detect the potential meat eater whose self-restraint and moral sense may not be strong enough to contend with the pleasure of wielding real power and the feeling of superiority that goes with it.

As for the potential grass eater, my impression is that most young American men who want to be police officers are looking for the pleasure of feeling powerful, special, and important. So when the opportunity to have his special position validated presents itself, it will be difficult for him to deny himself that pleasurable feeling. The difference between him and his meat-eating colleague is that he is far more likely to suffer from superego anxiety because his conscience is accusing him of wrongdoing. As a result, the grass eater will rely on defense mechanisms like rationalization and projection to cope with anxiety.

When a police officer explains accepting a gratuity or small bribe, he is likely to say something like, "It just goes with the job," or, "Everybody does it—it's always been that way," or, "It doesn't hurt anybody;" these are examples of rationalization. When he says, "It makes them feel better to give, so I accept," he is using projection. These explanations are attempts to soothe the accusations of his superego for having violated its rules. The meat eater has no need to use defense mechanisms because he has turned off the volume of his superego. He is not listening to its accusations and so has no need to defend himself. However, the meat eater may have a multitude of rationalizations and projections once he is caught.

POLICE BRUTALITY

The problem of police brutality seems to have become a major cause of concern with the advent of the civil rights movement in the 1960s. Since that time the term "police brutality" has come to connote physical violence by police against racial or ethnic minorities. However, Reiss (1980) noted that his research found that police were twice as likely to use excessive force against whites than blacks. The critical determinant in the use of excessive physical force by police, Reiss concluded, was the civilian's actual or perceived defiance of the officer's authority. The individual, almost invariably male, who challenged the cop's superior status was the one who was most likely to be struck.

In Van Maanen's (1977) description, this defiant male is labeled an "asshole" in the street cop's argot as opposed to the law-abiding but incompetent "know-nothing" who comprises the vast majority of civilians.

The asshole is the cop fighter who assaults the officer, the openly hostile loudmouth who perceives the cop as a malevolent parent and who also gratifies his exhibitionistic needs by making his challenge before an audience of onlookers. The asshole is also the overtly contemptuous civilian who regards the officer as an inferior who can be intimidated by mentioning some influential politician or who can be dismissed with the wave of a hand holding out some dollar bills. It is accepted among the police fraternity that the cop fighter not only deserves to be worked over but requires it (Burnham, 1973). The subcultural rules also say the loudmouth who tries to humiliate the officer by defying his power needs to be taught a lesson in proper decorum in the presence of a policeman (MacDonald, 1985). Neither the public nor the police department reacts with concern when the cop fighter or loudmouth complain that they were beaten by police. These individuals are regarded as bad people who should be punished with a beating for their behavior.

What then constitutes police brutality as opposed to the tacitly condoned use of excessive force on assholes? Perhaps the boundary between the two has to do with the policeman's criteria for determining who is and is not an asshole. When the officer uses the covertly accepted diagnostic procedure to label a civilian an asshole, then society and the department cast the proverbial blind eye to his roughing up a citizen. However, when the officer's criteria for determining that an individual is an asshole are too broad or not sufficiently rigorous, then both the public and the department are quite likely to accuse him of brutality.

Since the rules for deciding who is an asshole are very clear, how does it happen that the policeman does not apply them correctly? How does he too frequently mistake a citizen for an asshole? Part of the answer to these questions lies in the officer's unconscious emotional reaction to the work, as was discussed in Chapter 5. Every policeman has an unconscious ambivalent reaction to the job. He hates it because he is subjected to degradation and depravity and cannot do anything to stop it. His beliefs in morality and human dignity are under frequent attack by the misery he sees. On the other hand, he also has a powerful unconscious feeling of excitement and pleasure from mastering danger and exercising real, physical power over others.

Some policemen try to deny the emotional impact of the misery they experience by using projection as a defense against anxiety. For example, the policeman who feels overwhelmed by the degradation and suffering he witnesses may unconsciously defend himself from feeling helpless to deny his own unacceptable feelings of helplessness and anxiety by consciously feeling superior to the predators and victims who surround him. The policeman now regards himself as human and the civilians as subhuman (Waegel, 1984). He is virtuous and powerful; they are immoral and weak.

If they are totally undeserving of his respect because they are not human, and if their very presence constitutes a threat to his value system, his self-esteem, and his physical well being, then it is easy for him to define all of them as assholes in one form or another. The result of his all-inclusive definition of "asshole" is that this category becomes huge while the category of relatively innocuous "know-nothings" becomes very small.

Now the policeman tolerates nothing except total compliance with his orders and total submission to his authority. His feelings of superiority and contempt toward civilians as subhuman ward off feelings of helplessness created by the misery that surrounds him. The price tag for this psychological defense is his inability to differentiate the decent person from the asshole. The result is that he is very likely to feel justified dispensing his own brand of curbside justice to anyone who does not immediately submit to his power, since such a person must be an asshole. The officer is at this point defining himself by his power, and he needs to use it constantly to ward off feeling helpless.

There is another type of officer, described in Chapter 5, who copes with his ambivalent response to the street by using a different defense. This policeman consciously feels only pleasure from being powerful and brave while remaining oblivious to the unconscious anxiety he feels from his exposure to human misery on a grand scale. Unlike his opposite number who consciously feels only hatred for the work, this man consciously feels the job gives him excitement and a sense of pleasure from being "The Man" in the street.

For the policeman who is literally in love with the job, the street is a limitless resource of gratification. But in order to get the pleasure it has to offer, he needs action. A quiet tour is both frustrating and depriving because he gets no opportunity to feel the rush of excitement and pleasure in confronting and mastering danger. Consequently this officer needs to have action to feel the rush, and if there is nothing exciting going on, he will feel the urge to create an exciting situation.

All too often this means making a routine encounter into something bigger by seeing potential danger where there is none. So, in many cases a traffic summons becomes a search, the search results in disorderly conduct which leads to resisting arrest, and resisting arrest becomes assaulting a police officer, with the officer using force to defend himself. This type of policeman is notorious for converting a minor offense into a felony arrest simply because he unconsciously sought to create the excitement of being in danger and being powerful enough to master it, often using much more force than was originally required to handle the situation.

These men are not sadistic. They do not consciously seek to harm others as a way of gaining pleasure. Instead, they need to feel the rush of being strong and brave by mastering danger. The result may be that they use force when none is required, or they use a great deal of force when far less is sufficient. Thus the psychological impact of power and danger on the policeman's unconscious mind, and how he copes with them, may have an important role to play in the use of excessive force.

Clinical Reactions to the Effects of Police Work

One of the basic tenets of the psychodynamic model is that behavior is overdetermined. This means that there is almost always more than one cause of someone's overt behavior, so there are invariably several causes underlying a particular act. In essence, we must regard behavior as very much like a bill passed in Congress: every committee having something to do with the bill has some input; lobbyists influence the legislators to vote for or against it; both houses have to accept its provisions through compromise; the executive must sign it; and the judiciary must not question its legality. Consequently, the bill is the product of the influence of all these groups, which often conflict with each other for dominance, and its passage is the outcome of conflict and compromise among them. In the same way behavior is the result of the interaction of several causes that may compete with each other for expression. It reflects the influence, conflicts and compromise among the id, ego and superego.

The importance of overdetermination is particularly apparent in examining maladaptive behavior. There are very few instances in which symptomatic behavior is caused by one unconscious impulse, thought, or feeling. As the unconscious aspects of symptoms are uncovered, more than one unconscious cause is revealed.

Since the influence of police work on maladaptive behavior is discussed in this chapter, the reader should remember that a policeman's behavioral response to the emotional impact of the job is the product of the interaction of his personality's strengths and weaknesses as well as the actual influence of the emotional experience of being a police officer. This is why some officers' behavioral reactions are adaptive and others' are not. This is also why not all officers develop the same symptoms when unconscious conflicts become too powerful for their ego to manage.

The emotional impact of police work is complex and powerful, sometimes more powerful than the officer's psychological defenses to cope with it. When the ego's defense mechanisms fail to keep threatening impulses, thoughts, and feelings in check, then the individual's behavior changes in response to the potential intrusion of these unwanted thoughts and feelings into conscious awareness. Behavior changes such as these are signs that the ego is in danger of losing its ability to integrate and control the demands of the id and superego so that they do not impair the individual's ability to cope with the environment. In effect, these behavior changes, called symptoms, are maladaptive in dealing with external reality to the point where they jeopardize the person's psychological and physical well-being.

The major symptoms described in the police psychology literature are alcohol abuse, marital problems, and thoughts of suicide. Each of these topics will be discussed in this chapter. In addition to these symptoms, which are caused by internal psychological conflict, reactions to traumatic events will be described. Traumatic events occur in the external environment and are therefore distinctly different from unconscious conflicts within the individual. However, since they have a profound impact on one's psychological defenses, they cause symptomatic behavior changes in much the same way as do overwhelming impulses and effects from the id and superego.

ALCOHOL ABUSE

The abuse of alcohol among policemen is reported to be widespread. Surveys of active police officers indicate that problem drinking is prevalent in departments throughout the United States and Canada (Dietrich & Smith, 1986). Estimates of the extent of alcohol abuse are as high as 25 percent (Hurrell & Kroes, 1975). A disquieting statistic concerns the prevalence of drinking while on duty. Van Raalte (1979) reported that 40 percent (8 of 20) of the officers surveyed drank while on duty; Dietrich and Smith reported a study by Jones in 1980 that found 49 percent of the officers surveyed drank on the job.

While civilians may be surprised and disturbed by policemen drinking on duty, one officer observed that the street cop cannot avoid alcohol:

> If you had a couple of bars on your post, bar owners would welcome you to come in on your lunch hour or after work, and you pretty much drank for nothing. If you like the sauce, you had it all right there.

Another reason given for the high degree of alcohol abuse among police is the influence of the police subculture to drink as a sign of one's masculinity (Kroes, 1976; Babin, 1980; Captain Anonymous, 1982). Fellow policemen send the officer unmistakable signs that his acceptance as a member in the fraternity depends on how tough he can show he is, and one way of showing his toughness is his willingness to drink. While such peer pressure is obvious to anyone who has observed police interacting among themselves, it is a big leap from saying the subculture influences a cop to drink to saying it influences him to drink to excess. Placing the blame for alcohol abuse on peer pressure is a rationalization designed to relieve individuals from being aware of more distressing reasons for their reliance on alcohol, reasons such as painful or frightening thoughts and feelings.

Another reason cited for alcohol abuse among police officers is the failure of psychological coping (read that as defense) mechanisms to protect the officer from specific occupational stressors. Violanti (1981) regards "depersonalization" as a prime cause of alcohol abuse among police. He describes depersonalization as "a sense of individual self-estrangement, of one who experiences the self as alien. Through social interaction depersonalized individuals perceive themselves as objects rather than persons" (1981, p. 93). Violanti believes the police department is the chief architect of depersonalization in policemen. He says that policemen are trained to be emotionally detached from people and to behave in an unemotional manner (1981, p. 96). The result is that "impersonality is forced onto individuals who cannot help but feel human" (1981, p. 97), so that the officer experiences conflict between the department's demand for total objectivity and his own emotions.

The police officer tries to cope with the conflict between the department's demand that he be emotionless and the inevitability of having emotional responses by relying on what Violanti calls "mediation coping." The types of mediation coping used by police are cynicism, secrecy, and deviance. They are attempts to prevent the experience of stress by seeking to control its impact. However, rather than effectively mediating the conflict, these coping devices actually exacerbate the conflict because they create an even greater conflict between the officer and the department (Violanti, 1981, p. 227).

When cynicism, secrecy, and deviance fail, says Violanti, the policeman feels stress. At this point he relies on a "management style of coping," which includes the use of alcohol, "to manage the symptoms of stress after they occur" (1981, p. 120). Thus alcohol is used to relieve the effects of stress after the "mediators'" efforts to prevent stress have failed.

Violanti's view that the department is the primary source of conflict does not consider the intrapsychic sources of conflict proposed by the psychodynamic approach. His position, that the conflict between the individual and the institution is the dominant source of stress, regards the officer as simply trying to cope with the impossible demand by the department to be an unfeeling machine. The psychodynamic view sees the officer trying to cope with conflicts with both external forces, of which the department is one, and internal forces, namely, his impulses and emotions.

However, both Violanti's and the psychodynamic views agree on the use of cynicism as a coping device to ward off distress, whether it is called stress or anxiety. As described in Chapter 5, the policeman unconsciously relies on cynicism to ward off feelings of empathic pain and helplessness. When cynicism is no longer an effective defense against these painful feelings and thoughts, he is no longer able to ward off feelings of anxiety and depression.

Many officers for whom cynicism is no longer an adequate defense, or "mediation coping style," look to alcohol to alleviate painful anxiety and depression because it is quick, effective, legal, and approved by his peers as a sign of strength rather than weakness. Consequently, both views of the police officer's reliance on alcohol see it as a response to the failure of coping devices such as cynicism to ward off anxiety and painful emotions. In this respect alcohol is an anesthetic to kill emotional pain. Just as it serves as anesthesia for physical pain, it is relied on to alleviate emotional pain when psychological defenses have failed to prevent the onset of that pain.

ILLUSTRATION

Officer V. was a heavy drinker prior to becoming a policeman. One night on patrol he spotted a tenement fire and ran into the building to evacuate the building's occupants. Upon entering the burning apartment, he was told there was an infant in the bedroom. He ran into the burning bedroom, picked up the badly burned baby and administered mouth-to-mouth resuscitation as he exited the building. He drove the baby to the hospital. Someone asked him what was the dirt on his lips. He wiped his mouth and realized it was the baby's facial skin which was stuck to his lips. Officer V. then went to the precinct to turn in his gun and shield because he could not take another experience like this one. His sergeant convinced him to take back his weapon and shield, and told him to go home. To blot out his pain, Officer V. went on a binge that lasted several days. He became an alcoholic and subsequently was suspended from the police department for being drunk on duty.

Alcohol has another property besides being an anesthetic. It also depresses the central nervous system. This capacity to slow down the nervous system, "to calm the nerves," has given it the nickname of "the workingman's tranquilizer." My impression is that just as there are those policemen who use alcohol to kill emotional pain, there are other officers who rely on alcohol as a sedative to calm them down.

They are so stimulated during a tour in the street that they cannot readily leave the excitement behind and go home. They must tranquilize themselves after a tour because they cannot immediately go back to a less excited state. The importance of drinking to calm down is described by a police officer as necessary to reenter the civilian world:

> It's the recounting—that's why you drink. [Its purpose] is to unwind, recount or boast—it's to come down. The thing called the four-to-four tour, when you go to work at four, go to the bar at twelve, and close the place at four, is very common. You can't go to sleep if you don't. You have to tell it, that's part of getting rid of it, and the other part is drinking about it. It could be a sedation or a celebration that you survived another night.

The officer's need to reduce his level of emotional excitement and vigilance against danger is critical since he does not want to bring his mind set and emotional mobilization home with him. His failure to calm down before going home is labeled by many officers as "going home too soon." The following illustration shows the consequence of going home too soon:

> Officer X. had a particularly difficult tour which involved placing himself in considerable danger to make an arrest. At the end of his tour he knew he was still too hypervigilant to relax, but decided to go home anyway. While he was home sitting in his armchair, his wife sneaked up behind him and playfully covered his eyes with her hands. Officer X. instinctively grabbed her arms and flipped her over the armchair and onto her back. Despite his apologies for reacting without thinking, his wife was not amused or forgiving. After this incident, Officer X. made sure that he never went home too soon again.

A third property of alcohol is its ability to induce euphoria. There are officers who derive enormous gratification from the street and have either failed or never tried to defend themselves from its "bad pleasure." For these officers the watering hole after a tour is a place to prolong the pleasure of the street with the aid of alcohol. It is a place to feel special and powerful in the company of other officers and to feel sexually powerful in the company of available women.

When I first began to counsel police students at John Jay College, I naively suggested to a former officer that an after-hours facility at the college be made available to police officers who wanted to relax and to use the gym. He said if it did not have liquor and women, there would not be a cop in the place. "You see, the guys who are straight and narrow go right home to their old lady. The other guys go where the action is because they don't want to go home." It seems that for some policemen there is a need to continue the action after work with the use of liquor. As their reliance on alcohol to prolong pleasure grows, so does the potential for physical and psychological dependence.

ILLUSTRATION

> Officer E. was on street patrol in a high-crime neighborhood. He loved the action and the prestige of his position in the street. After his tour he began spending more and more time in bars and after-hours clubs in the neighborhood. He found that the excitement of his tour could con-

tinue in these places because the patrons knew he was
a policeman and offered him free drinks and treated him
as an important person. His dependence on this feeling
of being treated as important grew to the point where
he would go to these clubs on his days off because "it
was just too quiet at home." Officer E.'s absence from
his home led to marital problems. In an effort to save his
marriage, Officer E. gave up going to these clubs but suffered from chronic depression as a result.

Dishlacoff (1976) lists six psychological characteristics of
the problem drinker: (1) low frustration tolerance—he is im-
patient; (2) demanding of others—he demands immediate
compliance with his wishes; (3) extremely inflexible—he is always right and everything must be done his way; (4) perfectionistic—he must do everything perfectly; (5) judgemental
of others—he prejudges others; and (6) a good dispenser
and poor receiver of advice—he can dish it out but he cannot
take it.

These characteristics of the problem drinker are remark-
ably similar to those of Muir's "Enforcer," Brown's "Clean
Beat Cop," and Reiser's "John Wayne." Perhaps it is not a
coincidence that the men who need the emotional gratification
provided by alcohol are similar to those who need the emotional gratification provided by the street. If this is the case,
then the policeman who is addicted to the street seeks the
pleasure of alcohol because it is the next best thing to being
there. This is a third possible use of alcohol—as a substitute
for the high of the street.

Alcohol may prolong the euphoric state because it in-
duces a high similar to that brought about by the job. Indirect
support for this explanation comes from a survey conducted
by Jackson and Maslach (1982), which found that greater use
of alcohol by police was correlated with greater job satisfaction.

A study by Pendergrass and Ostrove (1986) sheds some
light on the relationship between the experience of being in
the street and the reliance on alcohol to cope with it. They
found that alcohol consumption was not related to occupational stress (internal affairs investigation, harassment, and

lack of backup) or divorce. It appears that work and family stressors were not related to how much an officer drinks.

They also found that alcohol consumption dropped among those officers who had been taken off the street and given light duty for more than three months. Pendergrass and Ostrove inferred that this drop in consumption was due to the officers not participating in drinking with fellow officers after work. However, another possible inference is that removal from the emotional impact of the street, whether painful or pleasurable, reduced the consumption of alcohol because the need for it to cope with powerful feelings no longer existed. If the cause of the policeman's emotional upheaval is the street, then when he is no longer in the street the upheaval is gone—and so is his need to drink to relieve emotional pain, to calm down from the adrenaline rush after a tour, or to prolong the "high" after work is over.

Thus the use and abuse of alcohol by police, like all other facets of human behavior, is neither simple nor does it have only one possible cause. A policeman's reliance on alcohol may be due to one of the possible causes mentioned: emotional anesthesia, sedation, prolonging the high of the street, or a mixture of two or of all three possible causes. It is comforting but inaccurate to regard alcohol abuse by police as the result of moral weakness or the department or any other single factor. The complex interaction of external and internal forces, difficult to isolate and very difficult to treat, are involved in excessive drinking, whether by police officer or civilian.

SUICIDAL THOUGHT AND SUICIDE

The literature on suicide among police is sparse, primarily because the police departments want to protect the image of their officers, and fellow officers want to protect the reputation of their dead brother officer and his insurance benefits for his family. The data compiled by the few available studies are contradictory as are the conclusions drawn from the data. For example, Friedman (1967), Niederhoffer (1967), Nelson and Smith (1970), Labovitz and Hagerdorn (1971), Heiman (1975), and Violanti and Marshall (1983) found the rate of suicide among police was higher than that of the general population, while Fabricatore and Dash (1977) reported a study by Dash and Reiser that found the suicide rate in the LAPD was considerably lower than the suicide rate for Los Angeles County. The small number of studies and the lack of consistent results suggest that this issue may be too hot politically and too complex to lend itself to statistical analysis.

Friedman (1967) used the "psychological autopsy" technique in investigating police suicides. He studied the lifestyles and personal characteristics of 93 policemen in the New York Police Department who committed suicide between 1934 and 1940. He found that 63 of these men manifested abnormal behavior and that two-thirds of this group were "passive individuals who were frequently of the quiet, reliable type, and in many cases, inadequate or inconsequential personalities whose suicide on superficial examination seemed to have no obvious cause" (Friedman, 1967, p. 429). The other one third of this group

> were of an overtly aggressive, impulsive and reckless nature. Those in the passive group had been predominantly functioning policemen who had some degree of adjustment prior to their mental breakdown and eventual suicide, whereas in the aggressive group the life plan had been one of maladjustment in relation to work, family and self. (1967, p. 430)

Seventy percent of the aggressive and 36 percent of the passive group were severe alcoholics.

Friedman's explanation for suicide among police is that it is essentially the displacement of murderous impulses onto one's self:

> The policeman is permitted to kill and receives praise from his superiors, peers and even the public for carrying out these acts. The aggressive and controlling drives,

which are no doubt the primary motivations for his
choice of occupation, are often in collision with the command to refrain and repress, therefore causing tremen-
dous conflict within him. (1967, p. 448)

The explanation of police suicide as the displacement of
aggression toward the self is too simplistic for such an overdetermined act (Heiman, 1977; Danto, 1978). The effects of the
job may be more involved than just providing the license to
use lethal force. One important effect may be discerned in
Friedman's two categories of passive and active personalities.
It is possible that the feelings of helplessness and empathic
pain brought on by the officer's being in the street may exacerbate feelings of inadequacy that were already present in his
personality, causing overwhelming feelings of self-loathing.
Thus suicide may be an attempt to cope with very strong feelings of "passivity," or, to put it another way, powerful feelings
of helplessness and emotional pain (Farber, 1968). Suicide may
be the "passive" officer's attempt to restore feelings of
strength and adequacy by taking an active step to prove his
courage and power still exist. Killing himself is his demonstration of strength, courage, and mastery, listed by Hendlin
(1963) as one of the seven unconscious motives for suicide.

As he is overcome by witnessing misery and human degradation about which he can do nothing, and when cynicism
and alcohol are unable to manage these feelings of self-hatred
for feeling impotent, then suicide may become the next and
last coping device to restore some semblance of self-esteem.
The act of dying by gunshot may be a sign of courage and
therefore a restoration of his ego ideal. Wambaugh speaks to
this issue in *The Glitter Dome* (1981). After a bout of impotence,
Sgt. Al Mackey tries to shoot himself with his revolver:

He stroked it again. This was the real danger. This one
he held in his hand, not the one that misfired in the
Chinatown motel. And look at it, the cylinder so rusty
with powder rings it could hardly turn. He couldn't even
remember the last time he had cleaned his unfailing cock.
Yet this baby never misfired.... He put the six-inch

Smith & Wesson service revolver on the table in front of
him. Lots of people are scared of their cocks. He was
only afraid of the one that didn't work. (p. 11)

The humiliation of sexual impotence, of the loss of sexual
prowess, reflects the impact of feeling overwhelmed by misery and degradation on the officer's ego ideal as the all-
powerful, brave defender of justice. The cop experiences
his powerlessness as a terrible blow to his fantasied self-
image as an omnipotent hero, which in turn causes him
to feel profound feelings of self-hate for failing to live up
to his ego ideal.

In this respect, the policeman's thoughts of suicide are
attempts to recapture some of his lost masculine power by
being brave enough to face a bullet—the ultimate proof of
one's heroism and strength. After feeling that he has completely failed to live up to his ego ideal, his willingness to
face death is a desperate attempt to restore his self-esteem by
proving that he is the powerful and heroic man he should
have been.

Friedman's description of the "aggressive" policeman
also provides a clue to the unconscious motivation for suicide
in those officers for whom the street has been a source of great
pleasure, so great that they have been unable to resist it. These
men have been seduced by "la puta," by the gratification of
their aggressive and sexual impulses in the street. For these
officers who cannot let go of such intense pleasure, there are
no ethical and moral restraints on either their impulses or their
behavior. The street has overwhelmed their conscience. The
straight life of family, saving money, paying bills, and taking
out the garbage is rejected for the excitement and action of
the street life.

Some officers feel they have gone over the emotional
edge and cannot return to the more moral but less satisfied
men they were before they went into the street. They may feel
that they have become tainted forever and can reclaim their
moral self-worth by killing off the uncivilized, impulse-
dominated men they have become.

In psychodynamic terms, their id has overwhelmed their ego's capacity to maintain a balance between external reality, the id, and the superego. The id is now too powerful for the ego to restrain. Thus the superego must rely on the harshest means possible to regain its position: the destruction of the bad, pleasure-seeking part of himself to prevent it from assuming total control. The only way this can be accomplished is by destroying all of himself. In this way, suicide is a desperate attempt to restore one's self-concept as a moral and decent individual after having given in completely to the bad pleasure of the street. It is the intrapsychic equivalent to the infantry officer calling in artillery on his own position rather than allowing it to be overrun by the enemy.

The police officer's motive is to punish himself for abandoning his morality and atoning for his sin. In paying the ultimate penance for surrendering to his impulses, the policeman seeks to reclaim his superego's approval.

A third motive for suicide given by Hendlin (1963) is to retaliate for feeling abandoned by loved ones. In this case, the suicidal individual is seeking revenge by leaving loved ones as he feels they have left him: in pain. This motive may also play a role in police suicides. Friedman (1967) and Danto (1978) conclude that marital troubles were the precipitating factor in the majority of the cases they studied. For the officer who feels powerless and overwhelmed by misery, his wife may be the one he turns to for emotional protection and feelings of self-worth. However, he cannot consciously acknowledge these feelings of helplessness and depression to himself, much less to his wife to whom he must be the powerful "knight in shining armor."

Consequently, he may become very demanding of her for nurturance while still wanting to be the boss. When his wife becomes unable or unwilling to be both the nurturing and compliant spouse he wants, then he feels abandoned by her. If he has come to see her as his last hope for feelings of adequacy and worth, then he may retaliate by leaving her and causing her to feel pain and guilt. Thus the term "marital

problems" may signify feelings of being betrayed and abandoned by the only person who could rescue him from feeling
inadequate and hopeless.

MARITAL PROBLEMS

Since the admission by the public and the police establishment that the job has an emotional impact on the officer
and his family, the police family has been viewed by many
as being under attack by the psychological and social stresses
of the work. Many studies have stated categorically that the
divorce rate for police officers is much higher than the national average without providing any data to support their
claim. Durner and co-workers (1975) surveyed officers in three
large police departments and found the divorce rate to range
from 16 to 33 percent. However, a study by Niederhoffer and
Niederhoffer (1977) obtained a divorce rate of 2 percent. As
in the cases of alcohol abuse and suicide, the data are skimpy
and contradictory.

Despite the lack of consensus about the divorce rate in
police families, there is nearly unanimous agreement that the
job imposes considerable stress on the family unit. Perhaps
the most significant stress described in the literature is the
change in the policeman's self-disclosure and emotional involvement with his family. It appears that after being on the
job for a short while, the policeman becomes more secretive
(Parker & Roth, 1973), more emotionally distant, and less involved with his wife and children (Reiser, 1974, 1978; Stratton,
1975, 1978; Hageman, 1978; Maynard & Maynard, 1980).

Two explanations are given for the policeman becoming
emotionally distant from his family. One explanation, by now
familiar to the reader, sees his detachment as a defense against
feeling pain and helplessness brought about by witnessing
tragedy and human degradation in the street. In an attempt
to keep these feelings from overwhelming him and harming
his ability to function on the job, the officer denies feeling

anything about what he witnesses. Since this defense is not readily removed when no longer needed, according to this explanation, the policeman perpetuates his denial of feelings and brings it home with him. The result is that he is in a constant state of emotional denial and his behavior is detached and dispassionate both in the street and at home with loved ones (Reiser, 1974).

This "emotional numbing" defense against feeling pain is employed by those officers whose primary experience in the street is one of feeling surrounded and overwhelmed by misery. These men are unconsciously feeling not only empathic pain and helplessness, they are also feeling angry at themselves for failing to meet the expectations of their ego ideal. These men consciously hate the job for what it has done to them and they unconsciously hate themselves for failing to be the omnipotent, virtuous men they hoped the shield would make them. They permit hostility to be their only emotion and malignant cynicism to be their only way of seeing the world. The reliance on hostility and cynicism results in both physical and emotional isolation from their family. Violanti describes his estrangement:

> The family soon becomes less important to the male officer. He becomes afraid to express emotion to his family or anyone else. Compassion is subdued in favor of "macho" image maintenance. As a result, the police officer begins to enforce his own independent brand of law, both at home and in the street. (1981, p. 63)

The second explanation for the policeman becoming emotionally detached from his family is that the family cannot compete with the job in providing emotional gratification. The street, "la puta," is more exciting and more pleasurable than the mundane role of husband and father offered by the family. Says Reiser,

> Because the young officer tends to become overly immersed in his policeman role, communication at home may tend to break down. Distancing occurs between him and his wife as he feels compelled to spend more time

with his peer group, to share his interests with them
rather than with his wife. Consequently she begins to
feel deserted, resentful and sees his job as competition.
(1978, p. 40)

Closely related to the street replacing the family as the
main source of gratification is the officer's changing attitude
toward his wife. In civilian life they may have been partners
who regarded each other as equals. The job changed all that.
After feeling the pleasurable rush of having real power, of
telling people what to do, and of compelling them to obey,
the policeman may unconsciously wish to maintain that feeling by staying "on the job" even when at home. He then sees
his wife no longer as an equal but as an inferior:

> Day after day and week after week the officer is con-
> fronted with people who regard his uniform and his pro-
> fession as the ultimate symbols of his authority. This
> continuous reinforcement of an officer's ideals can de-
> velop an emotional erosion which tends to allow him to
> forget or ignore his humanity whether on or off duty.
> The officer who is affected with this syndrome tends to
> become more rigid and authoritative with those whom
> he encounters, including his wife and children. His home
> becomes less of a domestic affair and more of an exten-
> sion of his squad room. Interpersonal communication be-
> comes difficult and those associated with him begin to
> resent his assumed divinity. His authoritative posture be-
> gins to override his good judgment and he experiences
> difficulty dealing with lesser mortals. (Ready, 1979, p. 40)

Ready's observation is similar to Reiser's description of the
officer's changed view of his wife. Where she was once his
equal, now "she is essentially there to meet his needs and
follow his orders rather than [as] an equal partner in a cooperative relationship" (Reiser, 1978, p. 40).

Unlike the officer who is trying to deny pain, helplessness, and shame for failing to live up to his ego ideal, the
policeman who is so in love with a job that he cannot leave
it in the station house is unable to control his basic desire to
perpetuate the pleasure provided by the job. In psychody-

namic terms, his id impulses are so strong that he cannot re-linquish them, even temporarily, to be a family man in equal partnership with his wife.

These two explanations for policemen becoming less emotionally intimate with their family, one involving hate for the job and for one's self and the other love for the job and for one's self, describe unconscious motives that are polar op-posites. Yet the behavior that results from them is for all prac-tical purposes the same. Whether the policeman is recoiling from failing to be the all-powerful, virtuous hero required by his ego ideal or whether he is in love with the work because it gives him so much pleasure, his behavior at home is one of aloofness, indifference, contempt, and hostility. The fact that both types of officers exhibit the same behavior at home poses a problem for his wife. How is she to understand what is the cause of his behavior?

One way to determine if it is pain or pleasure that mo-tivates his behavior is to assess how involved he is with fellow officers. In my opinion, the man who says he hates his job and really means it detaches himself from his peers as well as his family. He stays to himself most of the time and does not maintain his friendships with other cops (Neiderhoffer, 1967). The officer who loves the job prefers the company of other cops to everyone else, his wife included. He is anything but a loner. These men are animated and involved in their interactions with brother officers while being unemotional and uninvolved with their family.

A curious aspect of the problem of marital distress in po-lice families is the way in which the police department at-tempts to assist policemen and their wives to cope with the stresses of being a police family. Departments offer wives ride-along programs, seminars on the psychosocial effects of being a police officer, and information on stress reduction for their husbands.

In essence, the department exhorts the wife to cope with the changes in her husband's behavior by being supportive and understanding of his emotional distancing. While the department may also offer educational assistance to the police-man, it is rare for the department to tell its officers of the emotional impact of the work in terms of the pain and plea-sure it can provide, often at the same time. It is equally rare for the department to tell its men of the attitudinal and be-havioral changes these painful and pleasurable experiences can cause.

It is as if the department is denying that the job affects the officer's self-concept and ability to be emotionally intimate by saying it is the wife's rather than the officer's job to deal with changes in his behavior. Ironically, books and articles written by police wives (Webber, 1974, 1976; James & Nelson, 1975; Besner & Robinson, 1982) also place the burden of cop-ing with the policeman's behavior changes on the wife. She is told to be empathic, understanding, to give her man the emotional distance he needs, and to remember that it is his job which has made him change.

Perhaps if the officer was informed very early in his ca-reer that he should anticipate strong emotions to be a signif-icant part of his experience on the job, that he will feel love and hate for the job, often simultaneously, then he may be able to minimize the harmful consequences of the street on his family life. If he can deal with these powerful feelings, then his wife might not have to assume the burden of coping with his inability to handle them.

TRAUMATIC REACTIONS

In Chapter 1, trauma was defined as the overwhelming of the ego's capacity to manage threats from the external en-vironment, the id, or the superego. When the ego is over-whelmed by threat from the external environment, such as a natural disaster, an accident involving many deaths and se-vere injuries, or an incident that is particularly tragic such as the death of a child, the individual may react in a fairly pre-dictable way. In fact, enough has been learned of reactions to traumatic incidents to list them as a syndrome, a coherent group of symptoms, called the Posttraumatic Stress Disorder (PTSD). Posttraumatic Stress Disorder occurs in combat soldiers, rescue workers, survivors of natural disasters and accidents, and crime victims, as well as police officers. The primary symptoms of PTSD are recurrent nightmares of the incident, flashbacks (vividly reliving the incident while awake), intrusive recollection of the traumatic event, sleep disturbances, emotional numbing, depression, a lowered threshold for angry outbursts, and guilt about having survived when others died, or about the "immoral" or "unethical" behavior used to survive rather than to have done the proper thing and perished.

It is obvious that some of the symptoms comprising the PTSD syndrome have been described throughout this book. It is safe to assume that police officers who have witnessed or have been directly involved in tragedy have suffered psychological trauma and reacted by becoming emotionally numb, detached from loved ones, and easily provoked to anger.

Disasters, both natural and man-made, may cause police officers to have traumatic reactions. Feelings of being overwhelmed by the enormity of a catastrophe may have a significant impact on the officer's self-esteem. The officer's feelings of omnipotence and invulnerability are shattered by these overwhelmingly painful experiences.

ILLUSTRATION

Officer M. and his wife had been trying to have a baby without success. One day he responded to a maternity call to find a woman standing with one leg on a coffee table. Coming out of her vagina was an umbilical cord that led to the bottom of a wall. Officer M. saw the body of the newborn baby at the base of the wall. It was clear from the trail of blood that ran down the wall to the spot where the dead baby lay that the mother had thrown the baby against the wall and had killed it. Seeing the mangled body of the baby whose mother had killed it and knowing how much he and his wife wanted a baby brought a wave of nausea over Officer M. He could not bear to remain at the scene. He ran down the street, lit-

erally running into his own vomit. As a result of this
incident, he suffered a traumatic reaction and was placed
on temporary medical leave.

According to Mantell, "The emotionally perceived dis-
continuity between what the officer expects and what occurs
in a traumatic event is ultimately what leads to the development of [PTSD] symptoms" (1986, p. 358). To express
Mantell's statement in psychodynamic terms, the difference
between the officer's ego ideal and his actual experience of
himself is what leads to emotional numbing, detachment, and
feelings of guilt for not behaving like the all-powerful man
his ego ideal says he should be.

The officer involved in a shooting in which he has killed
a perpetrator may also show PTSD symptoms (Shaw, 1981;
Stratton, 1984; Stratton *et al.*, 1984: Solomon & Horn, 1986).
Again the dominant aspect of the officer's involvement in a
shooting is the feeling that he is not invulnerable. "After a
shooting, when one comes face to face with [his] mortality,"
say Solomon and Horn, "a greater awareness of what can happen often develops. One has to come to grips with dealing
with raw and basic fear and realize one is vulnerable and can
get hurt" (1986, p. 390).

Solomon and Horn also found that anger at the suspect for
forcing the officer to shoot was the second most frequent reaction. They believed that this anger was a defense against anxiety:

> Our observations are that, in many cases, underneath the
> anger are feelings of vulnerability and fear. In other
> words, the anger can be verbalized as "God damn you
> for making me feel so vulnerable." The anger, with its
> roots in feelings of vulnerability, can also be projected by
> administration, supervisors and fellow officers. That is,
> a person in crisis may look for a target to blame the sit-
> uation on in order to avoid feeling vulnerable, at fault,
> or out of control. (1986, p. 390)

Thus, the primary component of the officer's emotional response is the feeling of vulnerability which he regards as his
failure to live up to his ego ideal.

The anger the policeman may feel toward the department may be due to his unconscious need for the department to be the omnipotent, loving parent who can restore his lost feelings of security and invulnerability. After all, it was the department who gave him the feeling of being free from harm when it took him into the police family and conferred on him some of its omnipotence.

After a shooting, the policeman unconsciously expects the department to resupply him with feelings of invulnerability, but instead he feels subjected to further feelings of vulnerability by the department's policies of removing his weapon, taking him off the street, and investigating his conduct to determine if he was culpable. Given his needs, it is far from surprising that the officer is enraged at the department for being a depriving, rejecting, and malevolent parent rather than the nurturing, loving, and benevolent parent he unconsciously wanted.

If shooting a perpetrator in the line of duty is traumatic, then having one's partner killed is even more so. The feelings of guilt stemming from the survivor's belief that he failed to protect his partner are enormous, and can lead to severe PTSD symptoms. Here is the tragic experience of an officer whose partner was killed.

ILLUSTRATION

Officer K. and his partner responded to a burglary in progress. They entered a courtyard on the ground floor of the building that led to the main entrance. As his partner preceded him across the courtyard, the perpetrator suddenly emerged from behind a wall and shot his partner. Officer K. felt paralyzed by conflicting impulses to administer CPR to his badly wounded partner or to return fire. He decided to aid his partner, but when the perpetrator reappeared and fired at him, he did not fire back and tried to protect his partner from being shot again. Despite Officer K.'s attempts to keep him alive, his partner died at the scene. The suspect escaped. Officer K. was wracked with guilt that he had been a coward for letting his partner go in first and for not returning

fire, and that he had been incompetent for letting his
partner die. He was obsessed with having failed to ap-
prehend the perpetrator, who was arrested a few days
later. Officer K. refused to seek counseling because he
felt that anything he might say could be used by the
perpetrator's lawyer to get him off. A short time later
Officer K. suffered a nervous breakdown and was retired
on medical disability.

While the impact of major traumatic incidents on the
officer's self-esteem is easily seen, the fact that what are regarded as everyday incidents on patrol in an American city
may indeed be "little traumata" to his self-concept. In fact,
police work inevitably exposes the officer to numerous "small
tragedies" involving individuals or a small number of people
rather than to major disasters.

Although a single "little trauma" may not be sufficient
to produce a clinically observable PTSD reaction, many of
them may have a cumulative impact to create a PTSD-like
experience. The policeman who has been subjected to misery
and suffering on a regular basis may indeed be considered
suffering a form of PTSD (Martin *et al.*, 1986). He is easily
angered, emotionally detached from others, and depressed. In
addition, he suffers from a feeling of shame that he cannot do
anything to prevent or stop the tragedies he witnesses.

From a psychodynamic point of view, these officers have
suffered not only a severe blow to their ego, that is, to their
ability to handle their environment, but also to their ego ideal,
to their unconscious perception of themselves as omnipotent
and virtuous. In this sense the nature of the work is traumatic
to the officer in that he must confront feeling empathic pain,
helplessness, and shame.

Those officers who cannot cope with these feelings come
to hate the job and themselves for what the job has done to
them. They display many of the emotional symptoms of
PTSD: numbing, hostility, detachment, and shame. They come
to rely on malignant cynicism and projection of their own feelings of helplessness onto the public to try to restore the feeling
that they are still living up to their ego ideal. If their reliance

on cynicism and projection are insufficient to cope with the underlying feelings of pain, helplessness, and shame, then PTSD-type symptoms will emerge.

Those officers who can accept that they can never live up to their ego ideal because the shield cannot make them invulnerable and omnipotent are more likely to have the necessary flexibility to recognize their feelings of vulnerability and not reject them. These men have a better opportunity to cope with traumatic incidents, both large and "small." By acknowledging their feelings of vulnerability and helplessness to stop tragedies from happening, these men are affirming their humanity and their connection to the vulnerable and weak civilians whom they protect.

LINE-OF-DUTY INJURY

With the exception of having one's partner killed, sustaining a serious injury on the job is the most traumatic experience in police work. In addition to the obvious impact of the physical injury, there is also a profound psychological injury as well. The wounded officer experiences a blow to both his physical and psychological self-concepts. Every officer invests a considerable amount of his self-esteem in his body so that he unconsciously believes he is invulnerable to harm while in the street. He relies on this belief to put himself in dangerous situations without running away to protect himself, and when he controls his fear and masters the situation, the officer feels the rush of pleasure described in Chapter 4.

He also comes to take particular pleasure in his feeling of physical invincibility since every success in coping with danger reinforces this unconscious belief. Baruth (1986) quotes former NYPD hostage negotiator Captain Frank Bolz on this issue: "Put a cop on the job for a number of years, give him some success, and then put a bulletproof vest on, and he sometimes begins to think he cannot be hurt" (p. 306). A serious injury is traumatic because, says Reiser and Geiger (1984), it causes a

> puncturing of the officer's prior illusion of control and invulnerability. Inherent in the authority role is the assumption of being in absolute charge of one's environment. The officer victim is forced to acknowledge that another person has intruded into his or her seemingly inviolate space and interfered with the officer's control and autonomy. The experience tends to shatter the belief that "It can't happen to me." (p. 315)

The result of this shattering of the policeman's physical self-concept of being impervious to injury and loss of control over his environment is a lowering of self-esteem and feeling of shame. He feels he has lost the invulnerability he once had and can never regain it. It does not matter if he has always been aware of the danger of being injured. He has unconsciously believed it could never happen to him because he was invincible.

An example of this unconscious belief can be seen in the reluctance of policemen to wear bulletproof vests. The NYPD had a policy of not requiring its officer to wear bulletproof vests; the officer had the discretion to wear the vest or not. Quite a large number of policemen chose not to wear their vest because they said it was too hot in the summer or too bulky to allow freedom of movement.

In my opinion, these explanations were rationalizations to mask the unconscious belief that wearing the vest was submitting to feeling vulnerable and unable to master dangerous situations. In effect, the vest represented the loss of invulnerability, and these men would not allow themselves to relinquish their physical self-concept of being impervious to injury.

The unconscious need to regard his body as invulnerable may account for an officer's belief that policemen get hurt because they "fuck up." Since he is an excellent cop, and just about every policeman thinks he is after a couple of years in the street, he knows what to do and how to do it without getting hurt. In short, he will not fuck up so he will not get hurt. His body is strong and capable and his "street smarts" will keep him safe.

A serious injury crushes the entire framework of both his physical and psychological self-image. Gone is the firm belief in his body's invulnerability. Gone is the feeling that he has met the requirements of being omnipotent to satisfy his ego ideal. He consciously feels depressed and angry at himself for fucking up, but he unconsciously feels the very painful loss of his body's invulnerability and his omnipotent mastery of any and all danger. This loss leads to feelings of shame that he has lost what he once had. He is not the man he once was. Injured officers speak of their single wish to go back to the job and to be the man they were before they were hurt. What they are wishing for is to recapture their lost self-concept of being immune from harm.

At this point, the officer's fantasies of the police department's benevolent omnipotence come into play. He unconsciously sees the department as having the ability to restore his lost body image and self-esteem and hopes the department will cure him by telling him he is just as good as he always was, no matter how severe his injury. Instead, he is subjected to bureaucratic procedure and suspicion. The department's actions are themselves traumatic to the officer.

Instead of being comforted and cured, he feels assaulted by the department. Kroes (1985) says that the injured officer "is perceived by the administration to be malingering and is treated accordingly...adding insult to injury" (p. 82). The department's singular concern is the officer's fitness for duty, and its behavior appears not only adversarial but truly malevolent. Having unconsciously expected to be restored to his preinjury invulnerability, the policeman feels even more vulnerable and weak.

Kroes (1985) lists feelings of abandonment by the department as another common complaint by injured policemen. Not only is the department perceived as malevolent, it is regarded as having dumped the policeman, leaving him to fend for himself. "And the injured officer," says Kroes, "is treated like a liability, a 'pariah'" (1985, p. 82). It is little wonder that injured officers hate the police department for betraying and abandoning them instead of being the curative, benevolent parent they unconsciously hoped it would be.

In a similar way, peers are also viewed by the injured police officer as malevolent and abandoning. Wounded officers returning to duty often report that fellow officers appear to regard them with some degree of suspicion. This suspicion takes the form of the "reluctance of other officers to have him involved in dangerous situations because they are not sure that he can be counted on" (Anderson & Bauer, 1987, p. 383).

These clinical examples of the consequences of police work illustrate the enormous complexity of the psychological aspects of the job and the considerable difficulty policemen have in adjusting to its impact. The powerful unconscious forces of love and hate exert a great deal of conflict that is difficult to manage effectively.

Chapter 8

Some Modest Proposals

The great English writer, Jonathan Swift (1965), wrote an essay entitled "A Modest Proposal," in which he suggested that the Irish could reduce the famine then plaguing their country by eating their young children. The result was, not surprisingly, an uproar against Swift for his sarcasm and indifference toward the suffering of the Irish people. The title of this chapter is borrowed from Swift because the "modest proposals" suggested in this chapter may seem hostile to some.

However, these recommendations are the outgrowth of the psychodynamic exploration of the policeman's experience and are not meant to provoke a sense of outrage. Some of the suggestions may be regarded as impractical and even impossible given the current state of affairs in police work in America's urban centers. Perhaps they are. But their impracticality may be more a function of the mind set of those who have the capacity to implement change—be they politicians, police administrators, individual citizens or policemen—than the actual difficulty of bringing about change. Proposals will be made according to the groups to whom they are addressed: the public, the police department, the officer's family and friends, fellow police officers, and the individual officer himself.

THE PUBLIC

The American public needs to come to grips with its unconscious need to see policemen as parents. The police are neither all-powerful nor all-knowing and cannot make pain, fear and feeling helpless go away. Culver (1978) says,

> In spite of the misperceptions fostered by TV police shows, it may well be that we encourage their proliferation out of a need for reassurance that today's lawlessness can be controlled. By assuming the police are responsible for the prevention of crime and apprehension of criminals, citizen responsibility for conditions that encourage crime is lessened. (p. 504)

The policeman cannot make us feel totally secure from either accidents of fate or the antisocial predators among us. This need for police to be superhuman is both unrealistic and harmful to our ability to cope effectively with uncertainty and danger because it perpetuates our belief that we can create a world in which we can be happy children whose parents are taking care of us. Consequently, it is best that we civilians begin to rethink our own responsibility for maintaining public safety. We cannot leave the job of preventing crime and apprehending criminals entirely to the police, our omnipotent parents, while we do nothing.

We must become more involved in assisting the police by forming block watchers' groups to monitor movement on our streets and taking appropriate security measures in our homes and in our travel to make ourselves less vulnerable to crime. We must overcome feelings of isolation from each other so that we can be of mutual assistance in times of trouble. Now who can argue with these "apple pie" recommendations? Nobody can. These are relatively easy tasks for us to contend with.

The far more difficult tasks for civilians are to develop a greater understanding of ourselves and to change our perceptions of the police as our substitute parents whom we expect to make all our hurts and fears disappear. We must begin to be more in touch with those unacceptable wishes that we keep out of our awareness and to come to terms with them in a realistic way. For example, everyone unconsciously wishes to remain a kid who does not have to cope with the unhappy realities of daily life because there are adults to take care of him or her. This wish does not make us immature. It is simply an indication that life is hard, and everybody unconsciously would like to perpetuate the feeling of being secure and carefree. The problem, of course, is that we cannot realistically be more secure by believing that the policeman is our all-powerful parent and we are his carefree kids. We need to accept and to cope as best we can with our very real vulnerability to harm from which the police cannot make us immune.

Not only must citizens redefine the role of the police officer as an omnipotent, loving parent, they must also understand their unconscious wish to see the policeman as a cruel and punitive parent whose only purpose is to make them feel fear and pain. The policeman's job is to regulate citizens' behavior for the sake of the greater public good. That is fine with most of us as long as he does not regulate *our* behavior. Once he threatens us with punishment for violating the law, he becomes in our unconscious mind our heartless and sadistic bad parent who hates rather than loves us. We unconsciously regard him as our enemy because he does not leave us alone to do what we want, and we become his victimized innocent children.

This unconscious view of the police as malevolent parents perpetuates our self-image of innocent children who do not deserve any parental punishment. To the extent that we hold onto this unconscious belief, we perpetuate the feeling that the police are our adversaries rather than our allies in protecting us. The consequence of our refusing to accept our realistic adult responsibility to obey rules and perpetuating the self-serving belief that we are innocent kids who deserve only love and protection from our substitute parents, the police, is to refuse to come to grips with the reality that we must allow our behavior to be controlled because the world is not our oyster. We must give up some freedom in order to maintain our safety and the safety of others.

Self-awareness is far more than simply being more informed. It has to do with acquiring a more profound understanding of who we are and what motivates us to feel and act as we do. This is an enormous undertaking because each person must be ready to undergo a self-examination that few of us would do willingly and almost none of us could do easily.

In this sense the proposal that the public should examine its unconscious motives is like Swift's "modest proposal" since it undermines those psychological defenses that keep the child in us from feeling threatened. Self-examination would force us to accept the reality that the police are neither omnipotent, loving parents nor unfair, punitive parents. It would also compel us to recognize that our wish to see them as parental figures is based on our desire to be children who can be totally safe and blameless. Accepting this reality is more easily said than done.

THE DEPARTMENT

The department's ambivalence toward the policeman is no less difficult to resolve than that of the public. It would have to undergo major institutional changes to lessen the impact of the mixed messages it sends to officers. The effect of telling cops that they can and should handle any situation places them in the position of having to be perfect simply to achieve adequacy in the department's eyes. The result is that no cop will handle every situation well, so that departmental punishment is inevitable.

If the department is to lessen the stress caused by demanding perfection from its officers, it would have to make two major changes in defining the officer's duties. One change would be to do away with the all-inclusive role of the cop as crime fighter, paramedic, family counselor, dispute mediator, and psychologist. The department would redefine the cop's role by circumscribing his specific duties. In this way, the officer would not assume responsibility for resolving every problem he encounters and could "pass the buck" to some other agency.

This option would be practically impossible to implement because the police department would have to shrink to a fraction of its size once it starts relinquishing responsibility for certain problems. The amount of the police officer's time spent in responding to non-crime fighting situations has been estimated to exceed 75 percent. Removing many of these calls from the officer's responsibility would mean that fewer police would be necessary to respond to the remaining calls within their purview.

The department's budget, the size of its patrol force and its administrative structure, and last but certainly not least its political influence would be significantly reduced. The department would be cutting its organizational throat by implementing such a reduction of the policeman's responsibilities. It does not seem that any department would willingly undermine its size and influence to ameliorate the stress on its officers.

The second and far more realistic option to reduce the stress of inevitable departmental punishment is to change the department's mode of controlling the policeman's behavior from punishment to a system of selective reward and punishment. In theory, every department uses reward as well as punishment to regulate its officers' behavior. It can give commendations and promotions to deserving officers as well as punish those who do not follow procedures. However, medals and promotions are almost always given for crime fighting or for acts of extraordinary bravery, but not for a cop's ability to keep order and resolve civil disputes effectively.

To develop a system of reward and punishment rather than one of only punishment requires the department to give a higher priority to coping with problems and crises outside of crime fighting. The department would use commendations and promotions to reward officers for being extraordinary beat cops—for having the talent to keep the peace and maintain order without using force or making an arrest.

Implementing such a system would be very difficult because supervisors and high-level administrators would have to spend a great deal of time assessing officers' performance and determining appropriate rewards and punishments. They would have to function more as managers than as staff officers in a military organization. The department would have to redefine the administrator's role and retrain supervisors from sergeant on up to perform their role in a new way.

A second difficulty in rewarding the police officer for effective peacekeeping as well as crime fighting is that it may undermine the mystique of the police as heroic crime fighters of superhuman ability. If the police department gives rewards for outstanding noncombat activity, then it is telling the public that the policeman is not the Lone Ranger, he is a peacekeeper. This redefinition of the officer's role may make the public less in awe of the police and therefore less in awe of the police department.

Besides expecting its policemen to be always perfect, the department also treats them as if they were incompetent and untrustworthy. The organization runs along the military model whose underlying principle is that those at the bottom of the command structure know nothing and those at the top know everything. Thus the cop is regarded as mindless, lazy, and corruptible, so he requires specific direction and close supervision of his activities.

This departmental attitude incites rage and invites a retaliatory response consisting of the very behavior the department sought to prevent: doing as little work as one can get away with and not taking any initiative. It also provides the corrupt policeman with a rationalization for his behavior; he can always say that the department's mistreatment of him caused him to go on the "take."

If the police department wants to alleviate the anxiety of its men caused by its negative perception of them, there is one "modest proposal" available: professionalizing the job of police officer. The department would have to hire candidates who have a college degree, conduct an extensive screening to select only the most stable and mature candidates, provide an exhaustive training regimen that would screen out all but the most talented recruits, and require a prolonged field-training experience before sending the officer out on his own and giving him considerable discretion and nominal supervision. Finally, when a policeman makes a mistake, the department would have to support the officer's assessment of the best course of action and his subsequent behavior.

The department would be more than reluctant to professionalize the police for two obvious reasons. The first is the enormous cost of selection and training of recruits. It would cost a fortune and would be far from cost-efficient to spend money, personnel and time to eliminate the vast majority of applicants during training. The department would grossly exceed its budget and wind up with a handful of extremely competent, professional police officers.

The second reason is that the department would have to take all the political and social "heat" for the mistakes of its officers. By saying that its officers make honest mistakes in trying to perform their duty, the department is saying that it regards its men as professionals who cannot be automatically called incompetent because they make choices that turn out to be wrong. Needless to say, these two reasons make the option of professionalizing the work hazardous for any police commissioner to implement.

FAMILY

The "modest proposal" for the police wife is really an impossible one. Her task is to regard her husband's work as a job that has been invested with a great deal of mythology by the public and the police culture. She is to put aside the "knight in shining armor" myth and to regard him as a man with his good and bad qualities rather than as more special than other husbands. In addition she is to temper her feelings that she is special because he has chosen her as his woman.

Besides acknowledging her wish to see her husband as her "knight," the police wife also needs to be aware of her anger at him for shutting her out from his work experiences and for his emotional involvement with the street, her principal rival for her husband's love and dedication. To cope with her hostility, the police wife needs to face the fact that the impact of the job is powerful and must inevitably affect their marriage. She must make room for the job as an interloper in their relationship and accept the new "arrangement" that requires that she share her husband's love with her rival.

To ask a wife to relinquish some of the love she expects from her spouse because it must be shared with another is an incredible task. It requires that the wife concede some of her husband's love for the job and accept the emotional "menage à trois" that Niederhoffer and Niederhoffer (1977) have described.

The same "modest" proposal applies to the policeman's children. They must recognize that their father is neither a superhero of incredible ability nor an arbitrary and malevolent adult authority. We are asking children and adolescents, whose experiences are dominated by unconscious desires and fantasies, to be aware of them and to exert a conscious effort to keep them separate from a more objective assessment of their father. We are requiring these children to have a stronger and more mature ego than any child has.

FRIENDS

One of the most frequent consequences of becoming a police officer is the change in attitude shown by his friends. The old friend whom they knew has been suddenly transformed into someone they feel they do not know or like any more. Their unconscious ambivalence toward authority has intruded into their view of the new officer because in their eyes he is now no longer the friend they once had—he has become a loving or threatening parent.

As with the police officer's family, the proposal here is that friends must become aware of their own unconscious ambivalent feelings toward authority and to differentiate these feelings from those which result from more realistic perceptions of their friend. Once again, the "modest" proposal is that friends make rigorous efforts toward greater self-understanding to maintain a more constant and accurate view of their old friend who is now a cop.

The friend must give up important defense mechanisms to preserve the relationship. He or she must recognize that this newly acquired hostility toward an old buddy is based on his or her internal conflicts rather than on any real change in the new cop. We are asking for some very difficult soul searching from the cop's friend.

PEERS

The policeman's fellow officers are of enormous emotional importance to him. Their loyalty and support is a significant source of gratification he receives from the job. The officer's membership in the police fraternity is one of his most prized possessions. However, fellow officers must begin to recognize the high price they demand of him to be a member in the fraternity. They restrict the cop's acceptable behavior to a narrow set of aggressive, supermasculine, unfeeling, and nonreflective choices. In short, they are demanding that he be a caricature of the far more complex person he really is.

The proposal for the officer's peers is that they examine their own unconscious need to validate this caricature of themselves because it reaffirms their belief that they are omnipotent, heroic, and emotionally invulnerable. The caricature is so important to the police subculture precisely because it coerces every cop to be the tough guy to prove the image is real. Fellow officers can alleviate the impact of their hostility toward the policeman by examining their unconscious wish to be all-powerful and invulnerable and seeing it as just a wish, not a realistic perception of who they really are.

Peers must come to see themselves as having fears, doubts, "soft" emotions, and reflective thoughts about what they witness and feel in the street. Once they can accept themselves as being less than invulnerable, they can permit the individual cop to express his full range of thoughts, feelings and behaviors. He does not have to contort his complete personality into a narrow range of exaggerated attitudes and behaviors to remain acceptable to his fraternity brothers.

To ask the peer culture to give up the primary means of defining itself as separate from and superior to the rest of the population is literally to request a complete overhaul of the ways in which the police community establishes its identity and the way it derives emotional satisfaction from that identity. If you think this is a modest proposal, hang around a station house locker room or a local bar near the precinct for a while. The behavior of the police officer will demonstrate just how much pleasure there is in being the tough, aggressive cop and how important it is to follow the unwritten but very clear rules of acceptable behavior in the group. The idea of both engaging in self-examination to accept one's soft and vulnerable qualities and then to allow them to be part of the policeman's behavior is nothing short of blasphemous to the peer group.

THE POLICEMAN

The largest number of modest proposals are directed to the individual policeman. There are two groups of proposals for the policeman. The first group has to do with recognizing that he is the object of ambivalent feelings, attitudes, and behavior from the public, the department, his family, friends, and peers. The second group has to do with the police officer's own ambivalence.

Object of Ambivalence

Public.   The officer will have to accept that just beneath the surface of hero worship expressed by a civilian is hate for him not being the all-giving, loving parent the civilian unconsciously wants him to be. The policeman must rein in his own pleasurable response to admiration because it is neither constant nor unconditional. There are clearly a number of emotional strings attached to the civilian's affection for him. Consequently, he must try to accept hero worship with more than a few grains of salt.

Conversely, the policeman must accept that the knee-jerk hostility shown by some civilians is based on their unconscious experience of him as a powerful, cruel parent. In these cases, the officer may avoid angry and potentially violent encounters with these cop haters by not confirming their expectations that he is aggressive and punitive. While this is easier said than done, I believe that if the officer can avoid falling for the cop hater's baiting him into taking a threatening stance, he can defuse some of the civilian's hostility by doing the unexpected.

The old saying "You catch more bees with honey than with vinegar" applies in this type of situation, especially when the civilian expects vinegar. By appearing nonthreatening without giving up his authority, the police officer can turn the cop hater into someone less dangerous and easier to control.

Department.   In coping with the department's ambivalence, the officer has little flexibility or power to neutralize the department's attitudes of love and hate toward him. As mentioned in the proposals to the department, the expectation that he be perfect in every conceivable situation is not likely to change. Consequently, the policeman must live with the knowledge that he will be treated with hostility by the department for failing to live up to its perfectionistic demands. The cop must bear in mind that receiving the department's admiration, like that of the civilian, is not a sign of its enduring appreciation of him. The department will be quick to convert its reward into punishment should he fail to continue to be perfect in carrying out his duties.

In the same way, he must also control his anger at the department for its punitive style because, like the cop hater, the department expects him to be its adversary and will gladly take him on if he wants to fight. If he chooses to fight, he will surely lose in the end.

Family.   When it comes to his wife and children, the policeman must bear in mind that his work creates ambivalent feelings in his loved ones. They love and admire him for being special—stronger, braver, and more capable than other men. However, they are also angry at him because his work creates social difficulties with neighbors and schoolmates and because he seems to be excluding them from something central in his life. Leaving them out of his work life makes him appear even more remote than being absent when he is working night tours. The feeling that he is emotionally removed from them may be reinforced if he treats them as civilians rather than as his family. Giving orders and demanding compliance may make him seem the detached, uncaring man they feel he is.

The officer must be a civilian at home. He must be willing to listen, to compromise, to be affectionate, and to bring some of his important experiences home with him so that his wife can feel she is someone on whom he relies for support and understanding. He must also be willing to allow his children to have their say, to disagree with him, and to feel they can come to him with a grievance. In essence, he must leave his self-concept of police officer in the station house and put on his husband and father identity before walking through the front door.

This suggestion is anything but modest because it requires the officer to relinquish feelings of power and superiority and to accept a role in which he must be more accommodating, compromising, and emotionally soft. Only a saint can give up that kind of power to feel weaker and more vulnerable without believing he is making a bad trade. However, such a trade is necessary if the officer is to deal effectively with his family's hostility and to reinforce its love and admiration for him.

Friends.   The ambivalent feeling of friends presents the officer with a difficult decision. He has to determine if he can put up with requests to use his special status to help out friends, while at the same time be the target of their angry feelings toward the police and their attitude that he is no longer the friend they used to know.

The police officer must fight the feeling of wanting to withdraw from his friends because he cannot afford to sever his connection to the civilian life he had and must still keep. Failure to maintain his relationships with his civilian friends will result in his social isolation. He must put up with his friends' love-hate attitudes toward him because he needs to keep his ties to the civilian world. These ties permit him to remember that he is a part of the nonpolice society and remind him that his emotional experiences in the street do not necessarily apply to the rest of his life. Having civilian friends helps to keep him connected to civilian life and to remain a part of it.

Peers.   The ambivalence from his peers presents an enormous dilemma for the policeman. The love of fellow members of the police fraternity is of vital importance to the officer. However, that love comes with an emotional price tag. The fraternity demands that the behavior and attitudes of the officer conform to rigid standards from which there is to be no deviation. In a sense, the demands of the peer group are just as perfectionistic as those of the department.

The police officer needs to accept that he is an individual whose personal qualities may differ from those required by his peer group, and that his feelings, beliefs, and behavior may in the long run be more important than having his fellow officers think he is a man's man or a cop's cop. To risk reproach from the men who protect his physical safety and provide him with so much emotional gratification is certainly more than merely difficult.

The officer risks losing his group membership and the feeling of support offered by his peers, something he cherishes and needs. To suggest that he define himself by his own standards is comparable to asking an adolescent to give up his best friends and go his own way. When peers are vital to one's self-concept and emotional satisfaction, then the idea of risking what they offer to stand alone not only provokes anxiety, it causes real emotional pain. That is why suggesting to the policeman to think and act according to his own values, even if it means losing the love and support of his peers, is a "modest" proposal.

Police Officer's Own Ambivalence

The second group of proposals requires considerable self-exploration into the officer's own unconscious thoughts, feelings, and wishes. The officer must first accept the idea that he has simultaneous feelings of love and hate even though he may be aware of only one of them. Once he becomes aware of his ambivalence, he can try to modify its impact on his experience and behavior. These proposals require the officer to go through a difficult and extensive inquiry into his own unconscious motives that involves confronting and giving up important defense mechanisms.

Public. Policemen complain that they get little recognition and appreciation from the public for their work. They regard the public as indifferent and ungrateful. The officer needs to consider that his role of regulating the public's behavior leads to ambivalent feelings toward him. But he must also consider his own need for recognition and appreciation by the public as an underlying motive for having selected police work as a career.

If he took the job to receive public admiration, then he must accept the fact that his expectation was based more on fantasy than reality. He must face the unhappy fact that his work will bring him a great deal of hostility instead of admiration, and that people regard him with indifference or hostility when they feel they do not need him. The officer who feels betrayed by the public is reacting to the absence of emotional gratification he expected from it. The problem is that his expectation was based on his unconscious desire for hero worship rather than an understanding of the public's ambivalent attitude toward him.

The officer must also explore his hostility toward the public as his inferiors. He views the citizen with condescension for being less powerful and less self-sufficient than he. To examine the source of this attitude toward the civilian, the policeman must examine the effect of having power on both his self-concept and his assessment of others, particularly those with little or no power.

The officer must recognize that his feeling of superiority over civilians can lead to trouble if he does not remain aware of it and seek to keep it under control. The civilian who senses that he is being treated as an inferior by the officer may become aggressive to defend his self-esteem. Since the civilian is already carrying ambivalent feelings toward the policeman into the encounter, the officer's condescending attitude may validate the individual's hostility toward him and lead to an aggressive, perhaps violent reaction (Wellman *et al.*, 1988). The policeman treating the civilian who seeks assistance as a "know-nothing" or one who commits a violation as an "asshole" runs the risk of receiving a complaint or an assault as a reaction.

Department.   The department is invested with enormous power by the policeman's unconscious experience of it as both a loving and cruel parent. He sees the department as a vital source of love and security and at the same time as a powerful punitive adversary. In order to resolve his ambivalent feelings toward the department, the policeman must accept the reality that the department is a public service bureaucracy with real limitations, and that it is influenced by political, economic, and social forces that affect all governmental agencies.

Like the civilian who must recognize the policeman's real power and real weakness, the officer cannot expect the department to make him totally powerful and secure. The department is his employer, not a loving parent. And like the civilian who must accept that one part of the officer's job is to control his behavior, the cop must face the unhappy reality that one of the department's functions is to regulate his behavior with threats of punishment for mistakes or violations of policy. It is not the department's function to give him love or to validate his self-worth. The policeman who seeks love from the department is asking for the impossible and will be very unhappy as long as he unconsciously continues to want parental love from a bureaucracy.

Family. These are the most difficult proposals for the police officer to implement because they require him to accept the idea that the job is in some ways more gratifying than his family life. The predictability of family life, the requirement that he forego being a powerful authority at home, the necessity for expressing tender and soft feelings toward his wife and children—these make being a husband and father less satisfying than being a powerful, knowledgeable, and self-sufficient authority in the street.

The officer must be prepared to trade being in command and receiving compliance for being compromising, conciliatory, and emotionally open with his family. This is not an easy trade to make. The sheer visceral pleasure of exercising power is incredibly strong; therefore, renouncing that pleasurable state for being a partner to his wife and an emotionally available parent to his children is difficult. However, that is precisely the choice he must make to avoid being a cop instead of a family man at home.

Friends. After being in the street, where the extraordinary becomes routine and only the traumatic is regarded as unusual, the police officer has a tough time taking the problems and concerns of his civilian friends very seriously. Their complaints may seem trivial compared to what he has witnessed and experienced on the job, they appear to him to be ignorant of what life is really about, and they seem sheltered from the real tragedies with which he deals on a regular basis.

The cop's perceptions of his friends' nine-to-five lives and problems may cause him to view them with condescension. This reaction is understandable but it must be resisted for two reasons. First, his family are members of the nine-to-five world who need to maintain their membership in it. Should the officer reject participating in his family's world, he risks alienating them from the social fabric of their lives. Second, the police officer cannot afford to resign from his membership in civilian society. In the last analysis, it is the nine-to-five world from which he came to police work, and it is that world to which he must return once his police career is over. To reject his friends endangers his feeling of belonging to the civilian world and his reentry into it once his career is over. He will be a civilian for a long time after his membership in the police community is reduced to attending reunions of retired cops.

Peers.   The police officer is intensely loyal to his brother officers because he regards them as both his only ally in the street and an important source of emotional gratification. At the same time, he views them as competitors for promotions and better assignments and as potentially untrustworthy when it comes to backing him up or covering his mistakes.

The policeman must accept the fact that his peers are like most friends and allies in that they are valued for their support and love but they can never be totally supportive, trustworthy, and noncompetitive. Police friendships are intense because each cop relies on the other for his personal safety. In this way they may be more gratifying than civilian friendships.

However, the officer must realize that all friendships—no matter how intense—have a certain amount of rivalry, envy and mistrust mixed in with love and trust. His relationships with his peers are no exception. He should accept that his mixed feelings of love, loyalty, rivalry, and distrust for brother officers are the natural order of things. Therefore, he ought not be anxious if he feels both positive and negative feelings for them.

The Work.   Every cop both loves and hates the job. The street attacks his values and beliefs in the dignity of man. He is overwhelmed by the acts of cruelty and degradation people are willing to inflict on others or on themselves. At the same time, he is "turned on" by the street because of the intense pleasure that its excitement and danger give him.

The most "modest" proposal offered in this chapter is that the officer must reconcile the pain and pleasure provided by the street without becoming captive to either one. Like the sailor in Greek mythology, he must guide his emotional ship between the rocks of pain and helplessness on one side and of addictive pleasure on the other. To steer too close to one or the other means he will sink. If he is overtaken by the misery of the street, he will rely on malignant cynicism or alcohol to ease the pain. If he steers too close to the pleasure of the street, he will not want to leave it and will become its willing prisoner.

The police officer must accept the inevitable influence of both hate and love for the work if he is to steer a safe course through his experiences in the street. He needs to recognize that he cannot always protect others from tragedy or keep himself from being affected by the suffering he witnesses. He also needs to accept the unhappy truth that the capacity for cruelty and self-destruction is in every human being; if nature had to recall all its defective units from the assembly line, every person would be in the repair shop.

But this set of resolutions is only half of the officer's task. The other half involves recognizing that he is gratified by the street. The street provides the extremely rare opportunity to wield great personal power, to meet real physical danger, and to test both one's ingenuity and bravery. Given the fact that there are very few opportunities in modern civilization to do that while being paid for it, it is no wonder then that once a man gets a taste of that pleasurable excitement, he wants more and more of it.

It is here the policeman faces the most demanding challenge: to let go of that state of intense excitement and pleasure and to return to the far less exciting world of home, family, bills, mortgage, and the other ordinary aspects of life away from the job. In letting go of the attraction of the street, the officer must accept something in his own nature—that he is not different from other men. What makes him different from others is not that he has personal attributes that civilians lack, but that his job permits him to go beyond the rules of conventional social behavior—to exert power over others, to use physical force on others, and to enter dangerous situations to make them safe. Therefore, the policeman must accept the fact that he is a relatively ordinary man who, because of his work, has extraordinary experiences that affect his values and self-concept and that reveal his soul to him.

References

American Psychiatric Association. (1980). *Diagnostic and Statistical Manual of Mental Disorders*. (3rd ed.). Washington, DC: American Psychiatric Association.

Anderson, W., and Bauer, B. (1987). Law enforcement officers: The consequences of exposure to violence. *Journal of Counseling and Development, 65*, 381–384.

Anson, R. H., and Bloom, M. E. (1988). Police stress in an occupational context. *Journal of Police Science and Administration, 16*(4), 229–235.

Anson, R. H., Mann, J. D., and Sherman, D. (1986). Niederhoffer's cynicism scale: reliability and beyond. *Journal of Criminal Justice, 14*, 295–305.

Arcuri, A. F. (1976). Police pride and self-esteem: Indications of future occupational changes. *Journal of Police Science and Administration, 4*(4), 436–444.

Arcuri, A. F. (1977). You can't take fingerprints off water: Police officers' view toward "cop" television shows. *Human Relations, 3*(1), 237–247.

Aultman, M. G. (1976). A social psychological approach to police corruption. *Journal of Criminal Justice, 4*, 323–332.

Babin, M. (1980). Perceiving self-destructive responses to stress: Suicide and alcoholism. *RCMP Gazette, 42*(7–8), 20–22.

Bahn, C. (1975). The psychology of police corruption: socialization of the corrupt. *Police Journal*, *48*(Jan), 30–36.

Baker, M. (1986). *Cops: Their Lives in Their Own Words.* New York: New American Library.

Balch, R. W. (1972). The police personality: Fact or fiction? *Journal of Criminal Law, Criminology and Police Science*, *63*(1), 106–118.

Barker, T. (1976). *Peer Group Support for Occupational Deviance in Police Agencies.* Unpublished doctoral dissertation, Mississippi State University.

Bartol, C. R. (1982). Psychological characteristics of small-town police officers. *Journal of Police Science and Administration*, *10*(1), 58–63.

Baruth, C.L. (1986). Pre-critical incident involvement by psychologist. In J.T. Reese and H.A. Goldstein (Eds.), *Psychological Services for Law Enforcement*, pp 305–310. Washington, DC: U.S. Government Printing Office.

Bateson, G. (1960). Minimal requirements for a theory of schizophrenia. *Archives of General Psychiatry*, *2*, 477–491.

Bennett, Sandler, G., and Mintz, E. (1974). Police organizations: their changing internal and external relationships. *Journal of Police Science and Administration*, *2*(4), 458–463.

Besner, H. F., and Robinson, S. J. (1982). *Understanding and Solving Your Police Marriage Problems.* Springfield, IL: Charles C. Thomas.

Bianchi, F. P. (1973). *A Study of Psychological Characteristics of Law Enforcement Officers and Students Majoring in Law Enforcement and Correction.* Unpublished doctoral dissertation, University of Washington.

Bittner, E. (1975). The capacity to use force as the core of police role. In J. H. Skolnick and T. C. Gray (Eds.), *Police in America*, pp 60–68. Boston: Educational Associates.

Black, A. D. (1968). *The People and the Police.* New York: McGraw-Hill.

Blum, G.S. (1966). *Psychodynamics: The Science of Unconscious Mental Forces.* Belmont, CA: Brooks/Cole.

Brenner, C. (1973). *An Elementary Textbook of Psychoanalysis.* New York: International Universities Press.

Breslin, J. (1973). The policeman. In A. Niederhoffer and A. Blumberg (Eds.), *The Ambivalent Force.* San Francisco: Rinehart.

Brown, M. (1981). *Working the Street.* New York: Russell Sage.

Broyles, W. (1986). *Brothers in Arms: A Journey from War to Peace.* New York: Knopf.

Burgin, A. L. (1974). *Organizational Socialization in the induction of New Police Officers.* Unpublished doctoral dissertation, Ohio State University.

Burnham, D. (1973). Police violence: A changing pattern. In A. Niederhoffer and A. Blumberg (Eds.), *The Ambivalent Force.* pp. 174–178. San Francisco: Rinehart.

Butler, A. J. P., and Cochrane, R. (1977). An examination of some elements of the personality of police officers and their implications. *Journal of Police Science and Administration, 5*(4), 441–450.

Buzawa, E.S. (1979). *The Role of Selected Factors upon Patrol Officer Job Satisfaction in Two Urban Police Departments.* Unpublished doctoral dissertation, Michigan State University.

Buzawa, E.S. (1984). Determining patrol officer satisfaction. *Criminology, 22*(1), 61–81.

Cameron, N. (1963). *Personality Development and Psychopathology.* Boston: Houghton Mifflin.

Captain Anonymous. (1982). Battling the bottle. *Police News, June,* 20–23.

Carpenter, B. N., and Raza, S. M. (1987). Personality characteristics of police applicants: Comparisons across subgroups and with other populations. *Journal of Police Science and Administration, 15*(1), 10–17.

Cattell, R. B., Eber, H. W., and Tatsuoka, M. M. (1970). *Handbook for the Sixteen Personality Factor Questionnaire.* Champaign, IL: Institute for Personality and Ability Testing.

Chandler, E.V., and Jones, C.S. (1979). Cynicism—an inevitability on police work? *Journal of Police Science and Administration, 7*(1), 65–68.

Chasseguet-Smirgel, J. (1985). *The Ego Ideal.* New York: Norton.

Coleman, J.C. (1964). *Abnormal psychology and Modern Life.* (3rd ed.). Chicago: Scott, Foresman.

Conrad, J. (1950). *Heart of Darkness* and *The Secret Sharer.* New York: New American Library.

Cullen, F. T., Link, B. G., Travis, L. F., and Lemming, T. (1983). Paradox in policing: A note on perceptions of danger. *Journal of Police Science and Administration, 11*(4), 457–462.

Culver, J. H. (1978). Television and the police. *Police Studies Journal, 7,* 500–505.

Danto, B. L. (1978). Police suicide. *Police Stress, 1*(1), 32–36, 38–40.

Decker, S. H. (1981). Citizen attitudes toward the police: A review of past findings and suggestions for future policy. *Journal of Police Science and Administration, 9(1),* 80–87.

Dietrich, J., and Smith J. (1986). The nonmedical use of drugs including alcohol among police personnel. *Journal of Police Science and Administration, 14(4),* 300–306.

Dishlacoff, L. (1976). The drinking cop. *Police Chief, 43,* 32–39.

Dodd, D.J. (1967). Police mentality and behavior. *Issues in Criminology, 3,* 47–67.

Durner, J.A., Kroeker, M.A., Miller, C.R., and Reynolds, W.R. (1975). Divorce—Another occupational hazard. *Police Chief,* 42(Nov), 48–53.

Eisenberg, T. (1975). Job stress and the police officer: Identifying Stress Reduction techniques. In W. H. Kroes and J.J. Hurrell (Eds.) *Job Stress and The Police Officer,* pp. 26–34. HEW Publication No. (NIOSH) 76–187. Washington, DC: U.S. Government Printing Office.

Ellison, K. W., and Genz, J. W. (1978). The police officer as burned-out samaritan. *FBI Law Enforcement Bulletin,* 47(Nov), 1–7.

Fabricatore, J. M., and Dash, J. (1977). Suicide, divorce and psychological health among police officers. *Essence, 1(4),* 225–231.

Fabricatore, J., Azen, S., Schoentgen, S., and Snibbe, H. (1978). Predicting performance of police officers using the Sixteen Personality Factor Questionnaire. *American Journal of Community Psychology, 6(1),* 63–70.

Fagan, M. M., and Ayers, K. (1982). The life of a police officer. *Criminal Justice and Behavior, 9(3),* 273–285.

Farber, M. (1968). *Theory of Suicide.* New York: Funk and Wagnalls.

Fenster, C. A., and Locke, B. (1973). The "dumb cop": Myth or reality? *Journal of Personality Assessment, 37,* 276–281.

Fisher, H. J. (1983). A psychoanalytic view of burnout. In B.A. Farber (Ed.), *Stress and Burnout in the Human Services Professions.* pp. 40–45. New York: Pergamon.

Freud, A. (1966). *The Ego and the Mechanisms of Defense.* New York: International Universities Press.

Freud, S. (1923). *The Ego and the Id.* Standard Edition of the complete psychological works of Sigmund Freud, Vol. *19,* pp. 1–59. London: Hogarth.

Friedman, P. (1967). Suicide among police: a study of ninety-three suicides among New York City policemen, 1934–1940. In E. Shneidman, (Ed.), *Essays in Self-Destruction,* pp. 414–449. New York: Science House.

Gilmartin, K. M. (1986). Hypervigilance: A learned perceptual set and its consequences on police stress. In J.T. Reese & H.A. Goldstein (Eds.), *Psychological Services for Law Enforcement*, pp. 445–448. Washington, DC: U.S. Government Printing Office.

Gilsenen, J. F. (1974). *The Making of a Policeman: Social World Constructions in a Police Academy*. Unpublished doctoral dissertation, University of Colorado.

Golden, K. M. (1982). The police role: Perceptions and preferences. *Journal of Police Science and Administration, 10*(1), 108–111.

Gottesman, J. (1969). Personality patterns of urban police applicants as measured by the MMPI. Laboratory of Psychological Studies. Hoboken, NJ: Stevens Institute of Technology.

Griffeth, R.W., and Cafferty, T.P. (1977). Police and citizen value systems: some cross-sectional comparisons. *Journal of Applied Social Psychology, 7*(3), 191–204.

Griffin, G. R., Dunbar, R. L., and McGill, M. E. (1978). Factors associated with job satisfaction among police personnel. *Journal of Police Science and Administration, 6*(1), 77–85.

Gudjonsson, G. H., and Adlam, K. R. C. (1983). Personality patterns of British police officers. *Personality and Individual Differences, 4*(5), 507–512.

Hadar, I. (1976). *The Occupational Socialization of Policemen*. Unpublished doctoral dissertation, Claremont Graduate School.

Hageman, M. (1977). *Occupational stress of law enforcement officers and marital and familial relationships*. Unpublished doctoral dissertation, Washington State University.

Hageman, M. J. C. (1978). Occupational stress and marital relationships. *Journal of Police Science and Administration, 6*, 402–412.

Hall, C. S. (1979). *A Primer of Freudian Psychology*. New York: New American Library Penguin.

Hall, C. S., and Lindzey, G. (1957). *Theories of Personality*. New York: Wiley.

Hanly, C. (1984). Ego ideal and ideal ego. *International Journal of Psychoanalysis, 65*, 253–261.

Harris, R. (1973). *The Police Academy: An Inside Observation View*. New York: Wiley.

Heiman, M. F. (1975). The police suicide. *Journal of Police Science and Administration, 3*(3), 267–273.

Heiman, M. F. (1977). Suicide among police. *American Journal of Psychiatry, 134*(11), 1286–1290.

Hendlin, H. (1963). The psychodynamics of suicide. *Journal of Nervous and Mental Disorders, 136*, 236–244.

Herr, M. (1977). *Dispatches.* New York: Knopf.

Hibert, S. B. (1978). *Social Isolation Among Police Officers.* Unpublished doctoral dissertation, University of Kansas.

Hogan, R. (1971). Personality characteristics of highly rated policemen. *Personnel Psychology, 24*, 679–686.

Hogan, R., and Kurtines, W. (1975). Personological correlates of police effectiveness. *Journal of Psychology, 91*, 289–295.

Holder, A. (1975). Theoretical and clinical aspects of ambivalence. *Psychoanalytic Study of the Child, 30*, 197–220.

Holtzman, H. (1980). *Organizational and Professional Cynicism among Police.* Unpublished doctoral dissertation, St. John's University.

Homant, R. J., Kennedy, D. B., and Fleming, R. M. (1984). The effects of victimization and the police response on citizens' attitudes toward police. *Journal of Police Science and Administration, 12*(3), 323–332.

Hurrell, J. J., and Kroes, W. H. (1975). Stress awareness. In W.H. Kroes and W.H. Hurrell (Eds.), *Job Stress and the Police Officer,* pp. 234–246. HEW Publication No. (NIOSH) 76–187. Washington, DC: U.S. Government Printing Office.

Jackson, S. E., and Maslach, C. (1982). After-effects of job-related stress: family as victims. *Journal of Occupational Behaviour, 3*, 63–77.

Jacobi, J.H. (1975). Reducing police stress: A psychiatrist's point of view. In W. H. Kroes and J.J. Hurrell (Eds.) *Job Stress and the Police Officer,* pp. 85–116. HEW Publication No. (NIOSH) 76–187. Washington, D.C.: U.S. Government Printing Office.

James, P., and Nelson, M. (1975). *Police Wife.* Springfield, IL: Charles C. Thomas.

Johannson, C. B., and Flint, R. T. (1973). Vocational preferences of policemen. *Vocational Guidance Quarterly, 22*, 40–43.

Kirkham, G. L. (1974). From professor to patrolman: A fresh perspective on the police. *Journal of Police Science and Administration, 2*(2), 127–137.

Klopsch, J. W. (1983). *Police personality changes as measured by the MMPI—A Five-Year Longitudinal Study.* Unpublished doctoral dissertation, Fuller Theological Seminary.

Knapp Commission (1980). Police corruption in New York. In R.J. Lundman (Ed.), *Police Behavior,* pp. 260–273. New York: Oxford University Press.

Kohut, H. (1971). *The Analysis of the Self.* New York: International Universities Press.

Kroes, W. H. (1976). *Society's Victim: The Policeman.* Springfield, IL: Charles C. Thomas.

Kroes, W. H. (1985). *Society's Victims: The Police.* 2nd Edition. Springfield, IL: Charles C. Thomas.

Kroes, W. H., Margolies, B. L., and Hurrell, J. J. (1974). Job stress in policemen. *Journal of Police Science and Administration,* 2(2), 145–155.

Labovitz, S., and Hagerdorn, R. (1971). An analysis of suicide rates among occupational categories. *Sociological Inquiry, 41,* 67–72.

Langs, R.L. (1988). *Decoding your Dreams.* New York: Ballantine.

Langworthy, R.H. (1987). Police cynicism: What we know from the Niederhoffer scale. *Journal of Criminal Justice, 15,* 17–35.

Lawrence, R. (1978). *The Measurement and Prediction of Police Job Stress.* Unpublished doctoral dissertation, Sam Houston State University.

Lefkowitz, J. (1973). Attitudes of police toward their job. In J.R. Snibbe and H.M. Snibbe (Eds.), *The Urban Policeman in Transition,* pp. 203–232. Springfield, IL: Charles C. Thomas.

Lefkowitz, J. (1974). Job attitudes of police: overall description and demographic correlates. *Journal of Vocational Behavior, 5,* 221–230.

Lefkowitz, J. (1975). Psychological attributes of policemen: a review of research and opinion. *Journal of Social Issues, 31* (1), 3–26.

Lefkowitz, J. (1977). Industrial–organizational psychology and the police. *American Psychologist, 32*(May), 346–364.

Lester, D. (1983). Why do people become police officers: a study of reasons and their predictions of success. *Journal of Police Science and Administration, 11*(2), 170–174.

Lester, D., Babock, S. D., Cassisi, J. P., Genz, J. L., and Butler, A.J.P. (1980). The personalities of English and American police. *Journal of Social Psychology, 111,* 153–154.

Lifton, R.J. (1973). *Home from the War.* New York: Simon and Schuster.

Mac Donald, V. N., Martin, M. A., and Richardson, A. J. (1985). Physical and verbal excesses of policing. *Canadian Police College Journal, 9*(3), 295–341.

Malloy, T. E., and Mays, G. L. (1984). The police stress hypothesis. *Criminal Justice and Behavior, 11*(2), 197–224.

Mantell, M. (1986). San Ysidro: When the badge turns blue. In J.T. Reese and H.A. Goldstein (Eds.), *Psychological Services for Law*

Enforcement, pp. 357–360. Washington, DC: U.S. Government Printing Office.

Martin, C.A., McKean, H.E., and Veltkamp, L.J. (1986). Post-traumatic stress disorder in police and working with victims: a pilot study. *Journal of Police Science and Administration, 14*(2), 98–101.

Maslach, C., and Jackson, S. (1979). Burned-out cops and their families. *Psychology Today*, May, 59–62.

Matarazzo, J.D. (1964). Characteristics of successful policemen and firemen applicants. *Journal of Applied Psychology, 48*, 123–133.

Maynard, P. E., and Maynard, N. W. (1980). Preventing police family stress through couples communication training. *Police Chief, 47*, 30–31.

Maynard, P. E., and Maynard, N. E. (1982). Stress in police families: Some policy implications. *Journal of Police Science and Administration, 10*(3), 302–314.

McDowell, C. P. (1975). Victims, persecutors and rescuers: A challenge to police performance. *Journal of Police Science and Administration, 3*(1), 33–37.

McManus, G. P., Griffin, J. I., Wetteroth, W. J., Boland, M., and Hines, P. T. (1970). *Police Training and Performance Study*. Washington, DC: U.S. Government Printing Office.

Megerson, J. S. (1973). The officer's lady. *Police Chief, 40*, 34–38.

Menninger, K. (1965). Are policemen supermen? *Police Chief, 32*(September), 26–27.

Meredith, N. (1984). Attacking the roots of police violence. *Psychology Today*, May, 20–26.

Mills, C.J., and Bonhannon, W.E. (1980). Personality characteristics of effective state police officers. *Journal of Applied Psychology, 65*(6), 680–684.

Moore, B. E., and Fine, B. F. (1968). *A Glossary of Psychoanalytic Terms and Concepts*. New York: American Psychoanalytic Association.

Muir, W.K. (1977). *Police: Streetcorner Politicians*. Chicago: University of Chicago Press.

Murphy, P. (1973). Police corruption. *Police Chief, 40* (Dec.), 36–37, 72.

Nelson, Z.P., and Smith, W.E. (1970). The law enforcement profession: An incident of high suicide. *Omega, 1*, 293–299.

Niederhoffer, A. (1967). *Behind the Shield*. Garden City, NY: Doubleday.

Niederhoffer, A., and Niederhoffer, E. (1977). *The Police Family*. Lexington, MA: Lexington, Books.

O'Connell, B. J., Holzman, H., and Armandi, B. R. (1986). Police cynicism and modes of adaptation. *Journal of Police Science and Administration, 14*(4), 307–313.

Orpen, C. (1982). Effect of job involvement on the work-leisure relationship: Correlational study among bank clerks and police officers. *Psychological Reports, 50,* 355–364.

Paolino, T.J. (1981). *Psychoanalytic Psychotherapy.* New York: Brunner-Mazel.

Parker, L.C., and Roth, M.C. (1973). The relationship between self-disclosure personality, and a dimension of job performance of policemen. *Journal of Police Science and Administration,* 1(3), 282–287.

Pendergrass, V. E., and Ostrove, N. M. (1986). Correlates of alcohol use by police personnel. In J.T. Reese and H.A. Goldstein (Eds.), *Psychological Services for Law Enforcement,* pp.489–495. Washington, DC: U.S. Government Printing Office.

Piers, G., and Singer, M. (1971). *Shame and Guilt.* New York: W.W. Norton.

Pope, W. R., Littlepage, G.E., and Ellis, D.E. (1986). Philosophies of human nature and policemen: study of differences between recruits and veterans. *Psychological Reports, 42,* 1335–1338.

Preiss, J.J., and Ehrlich, H.J. (1966). *An Examination of Role Theory: The Case of the State Police.* Lincoln, NE: University of Nebraska Press.

Pugh, G. (1985). The California Psychological Inventory and police selection. *Journal of Police Science and Administration,* 13(2), 172–177.

Rafky, D. M. (1975). Police cynicism reconsidered. *Criminology, 13*(2), 168–192.

Ready, T. F. (1979). So your husband is a police officer. *Police Chief,* 46(Feb), 40–41.

Regoli, R., and Poole, E. (1979). Measurement of police cynicism: a factor scaling approach. *Journal of Criminal Justice, 7,* 35–51.

Regoli, R., Poole, E., and Hewitt, J. (1979). Exploring the empirical relationship between police cynicism and work alienation. *Journal of Police Science Administration, 7,* 336–339.

Reiser, M. (1973). *Practical Psychology for Police Officers.* Springfield, IL: Charles C. Thomas.

Reiser, M. (1974). Some organizational stress on policemen. *Journal of Police Science and Administration,* 2(3), 156–159.

Reiser, M. (1978). The problem of police officers' wives. *Police Chief,* 45(April), 38–42.

Reiser, M. (1982). *Police Psychology.* Los Angeles: LEHI.

Reiser, M., and Geiger, S. P. (1984). Police officer as victim. *Professional Psychology, 15*(3), 315–323.

Reiss, A. J. (1980). Police brutality. In R. Lundman (Ed.), *Police Behavior,* pp. 274–296. New York: Oxford University Press.

Reming, G. C. (1988). Personality characteristics of supercops and habitual criminals. *Journal of Police Science and Administration, 16*(3), 163–167.

Rubinstein, J. (1973). *City Police.* New York: Farrar, Straus and Giroux.

Ryder, S. (1979). Half the power of God. *New York Daily News,* May 17, 1979, p. 62.

Saccuzzo, D. P., Higgins, G., and Lewandowski, D. (1974). Program for psychological assessment of law enforcement officers: Initial evaluation. *Psychological Reports, 35,* 651–654.

Savitz, L. (1970). The dimensions of police loyalty. *American Behavioral Scientist, 13,* 693–704.

Saxe, S., and Reiser, M. (1976). A comparison of three applicant groups using the MMPI. *Journal of Police Science and Administration, 4*(4), 419–426.

Schlossberg, H. (1974). *Psychologist with a Gun.* New York: Coward, McCann and Geoghegan.

Shaw, J. H. (1981). Post-shooting trauma. *Police Chief, 48*(June), 58–59.

Shealy, A. (1977). *Police Integrity: The Role of Psychological Screening of Applicants.* New York: Criminal Justice Center, John Jay Press.

Sheppard, C., Bates, C., Fracchia, J., and Merlis, S. (1974). Psychological need structures of police officers. *Psychological Reports, 35,* 583–586.

Shev, E. E. (1977). *Good Cops/Bad Cops.* San Francisco: San Francisco Book Co.

Simon, W. E., Wilde, V., and Cristal, R. M. (1973). Psychological needs of professional police personnel. *Psychological Reports, 33,* 313–314.

Skolnick, J. (1973). A sketch of the policeman's working personality. In A. Niederhoffer and A. Blumberg (Eds.), *The Ambivalent Force,* pp. 132–143. San Francisco: Rinehart.

Slater, H. R., and Reiser, M. (1988). A comparative study of factors influencing police recruitment. *Journal of Police and Administration, 16*(4), 229–235.

Solomon, R. M. (1979). *Social Psychological Determinants of Police Behavior.* Unpublished doctoral dissertation, Auburn University.

Solomon, R. M., and Horn, J. M. (1986). Post-shooting traumatic reactions: A pilot study. In J.T. Reese & H. A. Goldstein (Eds.),

Psychological Services for Law Enforcement, pp. 383–394. Washington, DC: U.S. Government Printing Office.

Sparger, J. R., and Giacopassi, D. J. (1983). Copping out: Why police leave the force. In R.R. Bennett (Ed.), *Police at Work*, pp. 107–124. Beverly Hills, CA: Sage.

Stenmark, D. E., DePiano, L. C., Wackwitz, J. H., Cannon, C. D., and Walfish, S. (1982). Wives of police officers: Issues related to family—job satisfaction and job longevity. *Journal of Police Science and Administration, 10*(2), 229–234.

Sterling, J. W. (1972). *Changes in Role Concepts of Police Officers.* Gaithersburg, MD: International Association of Chiefs of Police.

Stoddard, E. R. (1968). The informal "code" of police deviancy: A group approach to blue-coat crime. *Journal of Criminal Law, Criminology and Police Science, 59*, 201–213.

Stotland, E., and Berberich, J. (1979). The psychology of the police. In H. Toch (Ed.), *Psychology of Crime and Criminal Justice*, pp. 24–67. New York: Holt, Rinehart and Winston.

Stratton, J. (1975). Pressures in law enforcement marriage. *Police Chief, 42*, 44–47.

Stratton, J.G. (1978). Police stress: An overview. *Police Chief, 45*(4), 58–62.

Stratton, J. (1984). *Police Passages*, Manhattan Beach, CA: Glennon.

Stratton, J.G., Parker, D.A., and Snibbe, J.R. (1984). Posttraumatic stress: Study of police officers involved in shootings. *Psychological Reports, 55*, 127–131.

Swift, J. (1965). A modest proposal. In P. Pinkes (Ed.), *Jonathan Swift: A Selection of His Works*, pp. 477–487. Toronto: Macmillan of Canada.

Sykes, R.E., and Clark, J.P. (1974). A theory of deference exchange in police–civilian encounters. *American Journal of Sociology, 81*, 584–600.

Symonds, M. (1972). Policemen and policework: A psychodynamic understanding. *American Journal of Psychoanalysis, 32*, 163–169.

Symonds, M. (1973). Emotional hazards of police work. In A. Niederhoffer and A. Blumberg (Eds.), *The Ambivalent Force*, pp. 58–63. San Francisco: Rinehart.

Teevan, J. J., and Dolnick, B. (1973). The values of police: A reconsideration and interpretation. *Journal of Police Science and Administration, 1*(3), 366–369.

Terman, L. M., Otis, A. S., Dickson, V., Hubbard, O. S., Norton, J. K., Howard, L., Flanders, J. K., and Cunningham, C. C. (1917). A trial of mental and pedagogical tests in a civil service examination for policemen and firefighters. *Journal of Applied Psychology, 1,* 17–29.

Terry, W. C. (1981). Police stress: The empirical evidence. *Journal of Police Science and Administration, 9*(1), 61–75.

Thurstone, L.L. (1922). The intelligence of policemen. *Journal of Personnel Research, 1,* 64–74.

Toch, H. (1965). Psychological consequences of the police role. *Police, 10*(Sept-Oct), 80–92.

Toch, H. (1979). Alienation as a vehicle of change. *Journal of Community Psychology, 7,* 3–11.

Topp, B. W., and Kurdash, C. A. (1986). Personality, achievement and attrition: Validation in a multiple-jurisdiction police academy. *Journal of Police Science and Administration, 14*(3), 234–241.

Trompetter, P.S. (1986). The paradox of squad room-solitary solidarity. In J.T. Reese and H.A. Goldstein (Eds.), *Psychological Services for Law Enforcement,* pp. 533–535. Washington, DC: U.S. Government Printing Office.

Van Maanen, J. (1973). Observations on the making of policemen. *Human Organizations, 32,* 407–418.

Van Maanen, J. (1974). Working the Street: A Developmental View of Political Behavior. In H. Jacobs (Ed.), *Annual Reveiw of Criminal Justice: The Potential for Reform, 3,* 83–130. Beverly Hills, CA: Sage.

Van Maanen, J. (1975). Police socialization: A longitudinal examination of job attitudes in an urban police department. *Administrative Science Quarterly, 20,* 207–228.

Van Maanen, J. (1977). The asshole. In P.K. Manning and J. Van Maanen (Eds.), *Policing: A view from the street,* pp. 221–238. Santa Monica, CA: Goodyear.

Van Raalte, R. C. (1979). Alcohol as a problem among officers. *Police Chief, 44,* 38–40.

Violanti, J. M. (1981). *Police Stress and Coping: An Organizational Analysis.* Unpublished doctoral dissertation, State University of New York at Buffalo.

Violanti, J. M., and Marshall, J. R. (1983). The police stress process. *Journal of Police Science and Administration, 11*(4), 389–394.

Violanti, J. M., Vena, J. E., and Marshall, J. R. (1986). Disease risk and mortality among police officers. *Journal of Police Science and Administration, 14*(1), 17–23.

Waegel, W.B. (1984). How police justify the use of deadly force. *Social Problems, 32*(2), 144–155.

Walker, D.B. (1975). *An Empirical Study of Police Value Systems: Socialization and Selectivity.* Unpublished doctoral dissertation, Wayne State University.

Wambaugh, J. (1970). *The New Centurions.* Boston: Little Brown.

Wambaugh, J. (1976). *The Choirboys.* New York: Dell.

Wambaugh, J. (1979). *The Blue Knight.* New York: Dell.

Wambaugh, J. (1981). *The Glitter Dome.* New York: William Morrow.

Webb, S. D., and Smith, D. L. (1980). Police stress: A conceptual overview. *Journal of Criminal Justice, 8,* 251–257.

Webber, B. (1974). *Handbook for law enforcement wives.* LE.

Webber, B. (1976). The police wife. *Police Chief, 43*(1), 48–49.

Wellman, R. J., Kelly, R. E. and Trapasso, P. A. (1988). Predicting "accident proness" in police officers. *Journal of Police Science and Administration, 16*(1), 44–48.

Wenz, F. V. (1979). Death anxiety among law enforcement officers. *Journal of Police Science and Administration, 7*(2), 230–235.

Westley, W. A. (1970). *Violence and The Police.* Cambridge, MA: MIT Press.

Wilson, J. Q. (1968). *Varieties of Police Behavior.* Cambridge, MA: Harvard University Press.

Wilt, G. M., and Bannon, J. D. (1976). Cynicism or realism: a critique of Niederhoffer's research into police attitudes. *Journal of Police Science and Administration, 4*(1), 38–45.

Zamble, E., and Annesley, P. (1987). Some determinants of public attitudes toward the police. *Journal of Police Administration, 15,* 285–290.

Index